IT HAPPENED IN
NEVADA

Elizabeth Gibson

TWODOT®

GUILFORD, CONNECTICUT
HELENA, MONTANA
AN IMPRINT OF THE GLOBE PEQUOT PRESS

To buy books in quantity for corporate use
or incentives, call **(800) 962–0973**
or e-mail **premiums@GlobePequot.com.**

A · T W O D O T® · B O O K

The publisher wishes to acknowledge the assistance of Phillip I. Earl, Curator Emeritus, Nevada Historical Society.

Library of Congress Cataloging-in-Publication Data

Gibson, Elizabeth, 1963-
  It Happened in Nevada / by Elizabeth Gibson.
      p.   cm.
  Includes biblographical references (p.) and index.
  ISBN 978-1-56044-944-7
  1. Nevada—History—Anecdotes. I. Title.
F841.6.G54   2001
979.3—dc21   00-032574
                                                                      CIP

Printed in the United States of America
First Edition/Fifth Printing

Contents

The Lost City
· 300 B.C. ·

If it wasn't for the construction of Hoover Dam, the Basketmaker culture and the Anasazi that once inhabited southern Nevada might have been forgotten. Some remains of the culture were found about 1924, but they were not really studied. It wasn't until interested parties realized the remains would be covered by the water backed up behind Hoover Dam that extensive studies began. The site was excavated and studied before the waters of Lake Mead inundated the area. Following original excavations by Mark Harrington of the Southwest Museum, Donald R. Tuohy of the Nevada State Museum led an excavation project, calling the site Pueblo Grande de Nevada. Once the project began, dozens of buildings and petroglyphs of animals and religious symbols dating as far back as 300 B.C. were found all over the valley.

Extensive study revealed that there were four major phases of inhabitants in the fertile flood plains of the Muddy and Virgin Rivers. The first phase, known as the "Moapa" phase, occurred from about 300 B.C. to about A.D. 500. The Basketmaker II people lived in the valley during this time. Not much is known about these people because few artifacts from their culture have been found. They did not build houses but used natural shelters such as caves. They made dart points but instead of using bows and arrows, they used the atlatl, a device used to give more power to the throw of a spear. A few willow and yucca baskets made during this period have been found.

The "Muddy River" phase lasted from A.D. 500 to 700. The Basketmaker III culture was predominant during this time. They were somewhat more sophisticated than the previous inhabitants.

They dug pits to make homes so they could be sheltered from the weather. They used pottery for cooking and storing food. They also left pottery in graves—suggesting formal burial of the dead. They discovered the value of the salt that occurred naturally in nearby underground veins, and they dug tunnels along the veins to mine the salt. The Basketmaker III people used stone tools, such as knives and scrapers, as well as the bow and arrow. They supplemented their diet of wild game by growing their own corn, squash, and beans.

The "Lost City" phase lasted from A.D. 700 to 1100. This period is more easily studied because many artifacts from this era remain. Anasazi now inhabited the valley, and by this time, the Anasazi in southern Nevada were as advanced as their relatives who lived near the present-day borders of Colorado, Utah, and New Mexico.

Between ten and twenty thousand people lived in the valley during the Lost City phase. They occupied enough space to cover both sides of the lower sixteen miles of the Muddy River. They traded extensively, probably with tribes in the Death Valley area and in Utah and northern Arizona. Their main trade items were salt and turquoise, which was generally made into beads.

The Anasazi made better use of their natural environment than earlier peoples. They mined magnesite, which was fashioned into beads and used in pottery, and selenite, which was used to make charms and ornaments. Interestingly, copper ore was found among the artifacts from this phase too, though archaeologists have never found any finished products to help us understand what it might have been used for.

The men hunted deer, mountain sheep, and rabbits, with arrows made from serviceberry, wild rose, cane, and currant. They fashioned bows out of willow, juniper, and greasewood. They used flint to fashion arrow points, awls, and knives. Women collected mesquite pods and cactus tunas for food. They used salt to season and preserve food; they carried salt in net bags and ground it into small pieces when needed. They used brightly painted pottery to cook and store food and made blankets and overcoats out of rabbit furs. They wove fine textiles and dyed them various colors using pigments from rocks and plants. They wove fabrics from feathers and made sandals and nets.

The Anasazi also domesticated dogs—perhaps for pets, perhaps as a beast of burden. They left behind evidence that they cultivated crops and built permanent buildings. These two facts suggest that these people were sedentary, meaning they no longer traveled from camp to camp but settled in one place permanently. They built brush dams and irrigation ditches to water their fields. They grew many crops including maize, beans, squash, and cotton. They built both above-ground buildings made of adobe and below-ground buildings called pit houses. Some of these buildings had over twenty rooms. One very large structure had almost one hundred rooms and a central square with only a few doors. It may have been a fort of some kind, though there is no evidence that such a defensive position would have been necessary.

These people even had time for leisure. The Anasazi may have been Nevada's first gamblers; primitive sets of bone dice were found among their artifacts.

The final phase, known as the "Mesa House" phase, lasted just fifty years, from A.D. 1100 to 1150. For some reason, the Anasazi began to build houses on the ridges above the valley during these years. These houses were positioned 120 feet above the valley floor. Such a high altitude suggests that an enemy may have moved into the area at this time and these houses were lookout points. During this short phase, the people were still farming and mining turquoise.

Following this period, there is no further evidence of Anasazi in the area. It is still unknown why the Anasazi left. Popular theories suggest that drought, famine, disease, or enemies forced them to leave. They may have migrated southeast into Arizona or New Mexico.

In the 1930s, the Civilian Conservation Corps built the Lost

City Museum near the town of Overton, Nevada, to commemorate Nevada's ancient civilization. Today, the museum has one of the most complete displays of this desert culture. The museum preserves several Pueblo type houses that have been reconstructed on original foundations. Natural plants that the Indians would have used, such as mesquite and screwbean, have been planted for display.

Someday many more secrets may be uncovered when the many miles of ruins that still exist in Nevada are excavated and studied.

Joseph Walker Encounters Indians

· 1833 ·

In 1832, Captain Benjamin Louis Eulalie de Bonneville took a leave of absence from the Army to explore the American West. His goal was to map the West, as well as to scout likely fur trapping areas. The following July, Bonneville reached the Green River in northern Utah. From there, he sent out three scouting parties. He picked Joseph Walker to lead one of those parties.

Walker's assignment was to explore the area around the Great Salt Lake and regions west. He would also scout for the fabled River Buenaventura, thought to be a river outlet to the Pacific Ocean.

Walker handpicked thirty-five men, including clerk Zenas Leonard, to accompany him on the trip. Some Indians advised Walker to stock up on provisions, since once he got west of the Great Salt Lake, game would be scarce. Walker took this advice and was glad he did. He was more prepared for what lay ahead than he might have been had he not heeded this advice.

Walker's party crossed Nevada's eastern border near what is today called Pilot Peak. The group had barely started trapping in the area when they had trouble with the local Paiute Indians. Just as soon as the men could place their traps, the Indians would steal them. This was very much a concern since not only were the traps a significant investment at fifteen to twenty dollars each, but they were irreplaceable once a man was out in the wilderness. But Walker did not want any trouble with the Indians. He was content to just take the loss and go about his business. He even altered his route somewhat to stay away from the Indians.

Unfortunately, some of the men in the party did not agree with his pacifist policy. They sought revenge. Some of the white men killed a few Paiutes while out hunting. Walker was unaware of what they had done. On another day, some white men started to sneak out to fight the Indians again. This time Walker caught them and found out about their earlier deed. He was much dismayed. He knew this would lead to further troubles with the Paiutes.

Walker's party trapped along the Humboldt River as they traveled west. They rode quite a distance without seeing any Indians, and Walker began to think that they would be left alone. He and his party reached the Humboldt Sink near modern-day Lovelock about August 10. Before them was a vast grassy plain with plenty of forage for their animals. There was evidently plenty of forage and food for the eight or nine hundred Paiute Indians present as well.

Because the Paiutes did not look friendly, the white men assumed a defensive position right away. It seemed to Walker that they were out for revenge. He ordered the men to pile up some of their baggage to build a barricade. They hitched all their horses together and tied them to stakes in the ground.

Several Paiute chiefs came forward. They wanted the white "chief" to come into their camp and talk. Walker signed that he would not do this but would meet them halfway between the two camps. The chiefs did not like this response. They hurried back to their camp. A whole line of Indians surged forward.

Walker and several others warned the Indians to stay back or they would be killed. The Indians laughed thinking there was no way the white men could kill them with so great a distance between them. These Indians had never seen guns before, so Walker decided to demonstrate. He fired a warning shot toward some ducks standing by a nearby pond. The Indians were surprised when one of ducks fell dead but did not really grasp why this was so. However, they did hold off their attack.

The fur-trapping party continued south. Though battle had been averted, the Indians still followed the white men and hid in the tall grass all around them. Small groups of Indians periodically confronted the white men and demanded that they stop to smoke. This was a delaying tactic designed to allow more of their comrades to get close.

Finally Walker had enough of their taunting. He decided to teach them a lesson. Between eighty and one hundred Indians had approached, but even though his party was outnumbered by about two to one, Walker figured their firepower would make up for their smaller numbers. The men first tied the pack animals to some shrubs. Then they galloped full speed toward the Indians, and Walker signaled the men to attack. In just a short time, the white men killed about thirty-five Indians and the rest ran away. The white men quickly built some rafts out of tule rushes and sailed across the river and through the Humboldt Sink area.

Walker's party proceeded unmolested for the rest of their trip. By the time they reached the Carson Sink, the trappers were out of food and had to subsist on rabbits and the dried lake flies that the Indians ate. The horses did not fare well either. Somehow the trappers eventually got over the Sierras and spent the winter in California near Monterey.

Walker had more troubles on the return trip. He and his men got lost in the desert between Death Valley and Tonopah for several weeks with little food and water, and sixty-four horses, ten cows, and fifteen dogs perished. There was so little game that they ate many of their own dead animals. Walker was finally able to find their original track from their westward journey and trace it back to the Humboldt River.

When the trappers reached the Humboldt Sink, there were even more Indians in the area than had been there the previous year. Walker offered gifts to the chiefs, but the gifts did not appease them. He offered to side with the Paiutes and help them fight their enemies. This offer went unaccepted. So rather than risk being put on the defensive, Walker struck first. During a short skirmish, the trappers killed fourteen Indians. Only three trappers were wounded.

After this final battle, Walker's party continued on up the Humboldt River without any more harassment from Indians. Near the headwaters of the Humboldt, Walker took a different route to meet up with Bonneville. He headed north to the Snake River, then followed it to the headwaters of the Bear River.

Walker was the first man to lead a group of white men along the Humboldt River in Nevada. His route later became part of the route many emigrants traveled to California. Historians have praised him for his efforts to avoid conflict with the Indians, something later leaders did not always attempt. After retiring from exploring, Walker started a ranch in California, where he died in 1876.

Banished from the Donner Party
· 1846 ·

The leaders of the Donner Party made their decision; they would try the new route blazed by Lansford W. Hastings. Instead of following the California Trail from Fort Bridger, Wyoming, to Fort Hall, Idaho, and into Nevada through its northeast corner, the Donner Party would follow the new southwest trail through the Wasatch Mountains of Utah and across the desert to the Humboldt River in Nevada.

The Donner Party, so called because it was led by George Donner, left Fort Bridger on July 31, 1846. It took them over a month just to get through the Wasatch Mountains and another month before they reached the Humboldt River and joined up with the established trail to California. They lost many animals due to heat and starvation, and many of their wagons were destroyed by the rough terrain. They were worn out from heat exhaustion and improper nutrition. It wasn't too surprising that the people began to argue. One disagreement on October 5, 1846, led to tragedy.

Historians disagree about exactly where the event took place. Many accounts mention Gravelly Ford but disagree about where Gravelly Ford is located. At any rate, the Donner Party was driving along the Humboldt, probably somewhere between today's Winnemucca and Battle Mountain, when they came to a ridge that proved especially difficult to cross. The only way to get the wagons over the steep, sandy hill was to double-team the oxen to pull each wagon up the hill. Franklin Graves led the party up the ridge, and Jay Fosdick, his son-in-law, followed behind him. John Snyder followed behind Fosdick, driving one of the Graves's wagons, and Milt Elliot, driving James Reed's wagon, followed him. While Fosdick was helping Graves with his wagon, Elliott started arguing with Snyder. It is not known exactly why they argued, but it may have been about the order of the wagons. Another reason may have been that Snyder insisted that his team could make it up the hill without help. At any rate, the result was that Snyder began whipping his oxen. Elliot felt this use of force was unjustified. Just then, Reed rode up after returning from a hunting trip and scolded Snyder for treating the oxen so badly. He knew that without oxen, no one would get to California. Snyder didn't appreciate the interference. He had harsh words for Reed. An argument followed.

Reed tried to soothe the man and suggested they talk about it once they got over the hill. But Snyder wanted to have it out right then. He jumped up on the tongue of his wagon and swung at Reed with the butt of his whip. He hit Reed until he was bleeding severely. After several blows, Margaret Reed tried to intervene and got slapped with the whip for her efforts. Before he knew what he was doing, Reed whipped out his hunting knife and stabbed Snyder. The knife struck Snyder in the left breast, snapping his first and second ribs and piercing his left lung. Billy Graves caught Snyder as he fell and laid him on the ground. Reed immediately rushed to the man to try to stop the flow of blood. But Snyder died almost immediately.

Reed's daughter, Virginia, washed and dressed her father's wounds, since Margaret was too distraught to do it herself. Reed offered some boards from his wagon to fashion a coffin for Snyder's body, but the others rejected the offer. A short service was held at Snyder's final resting place. Reed regretted what had happened since Snyder had been a good friend.

After the funeral, other members of the party decided something had to be done to punish Reed. Some wrote statements suggesting that Reed be brought to trial once they reached California. Louis Keseburg wanted to hang Reed on the spot. He had held a personal grudge against Reed ever since Reed had stopped him from physically abusing his wife. Snyder was very popular, which probably contributed to the harsh feelings against Reed. At twenty-three, Snyder was a frontiersman with a gentle nature, who entertained others with his stories. He performed amusing jigs and dances for the party around the campfire. Others, envious of the Reed family's social position in the wagon train, may have resented their affluence and were glad that something bad had happened to them. Eventually William Eddy and Milt Elliot were the only persons fighting on Reed's behalf. Eddy suggested that Reed be allowed to leave the wagon train and go ahead. The rest of the wagon train agreed to this, and Reed was sentenced to banishment.

At first Reed refused to leave, saying he had only acted in self-defense. But Margaret urged him to go ahead, reasoning that he could go for help. At first the others insisted Reed leave his horse and weapons behind. They finally agreed to let him take his horse but would not allow him to take weapons or ammunition.

In the morning, Reed made arrangements for his family to be taken care of, bid them goodbye, and left the wagon train. After dark, Virginia and Milt Elliott caught up with him and gave Reed his rifle, pistols, ammunition, and some food. Virginia wanted to go with her father, but Reed wouldn't let her. She would have to look after her little brothers and sisters. So she returned to the camp with Elliott.

Reed didn't know it, but the other members of the Donner Party may have saved his life. By leaving the wagon train, he was able to travel much faster, and he quickly caught up with the Donners and others who were riding about two days ahead of the rest. One of Reed's teamsters, Walter Herron, who had been riding with the Donners, joined Reed for his lonely journey west. For a while, the Reed family would find a letter stuck on a bush or a stick and they would know that their patriarch was still alive. But after awhile there were no more letters, and the family began to worry that Reed had starved or been killed by Indians. It would be four months before they would know that Reed and Herron had easily reached Sutter's Mill in California.

When winter set in and his family had not yet reached Sutter's Mill, Reed began to worry. On October 30, he rode east with a rescue party but had to turn back because of harsh weather. He set out with another rescue party on February 22 and this time made it to the lake where the Donner Party had holed up to wait out the winter. Reed led several people, including his family, back to Sutter's Mill.

Of the eighty-nine Donner Party members who started west, only forty-seven survived. Miraculously, all of Reed's family survived, and the Reeds went on to be important figures in the development of San Jose, California.

The Pyramid Lake War
· 1860 ·

The Northern Paiutes had been a peaceful tribe, spending their time catching fish in Pyramid Lake and collecting pine nuts from the forest. They did not bother the families at the Honey Lake Valley settlement just over the border in California. Early on the settlers and Indians had made a treaty. The white men agreed to punish anyone who stole from or harassed the Indians, and the Indians, represented by Old Winnemucca, agreed to punish any Indian caught stealing from or harassing the whites. This agreement created a harmonious existence between the two camps.

This friendly relationship continued until the discovery of a great silver lode at Virginia City, Nevada, in 1859. People rushed to the area, seeking a fortune in silver. The newcomers treated the Indians cruelly. The Indians expected their agreement to apply to all white men and were surprised when it did not.

The Pyramid Lake War began in January 1860 when Indians killed a man named Dexter Deming at Willow Creek. The act was probably revenge against Deming's brother Jack, who was known as an Indian hater by both the whites and the Indians.

The whites demanded that the Paiutes surrender those who killed Deming. Old Winnemucca refused and countered with a demand of sixteen thousand dollars to pay for the loss of Paiute hunting grounds and the piñon trees that had been cut down by white settlers. Except for Numaga, all the Paiute chiefs favored war.

While negotiations dragged on, some renegade Indians attacked Williams Station, a Pony Express stop, on May 7. The reason for the attack is usually attributed to the fact that the stationkeepers had captured two young Indian girls and imprisoned them at the station. Three men were killed by the Paiutes in the attack.

On May 9, anxious citizens met in Virginia City to decide what to do. A group of volunteers formed, with Captain Archie McDonald as the leader. Meanwhile, another group of volunteers formed in Silver City, with R. G. Watkins, a former naval officer, as the leader. In Genoa, a group of volunteers formed under Captain Thomas F. Condon, Jr. A fourth group formed in Carson City, led by Major William O. Ormsby.

Ready to confront the Indians, the four groups started down the Carson River on May 10. The weather was chilly, the wind blew hard, and snow covered the ground. Ormsby's force arrived at Williams Station first and set up camp. By nightfall, many volunteers were having misgivings about continuing. The weather was bad and there were signs of Indians all around them. Some returned to town in the morning. Ormsby assumed command of the 105 volunteers that remained.

The next day, the volunteers traveled along the Truckee River into an area covered with sagebrush and camped there for the night. They saw no Indians. The next day Ormsby sent a scouting party ahead. When the scouts returned, they reported that they saw Indian tracks all around them, but no Indians. Extra cautious, the men rode along a narrow trail through a river gorge and down a steep sagebrush-covered slope. Then two scouts spotted two Indians and tried to capture them. But as soon as they started after the two braves, an entire war party appeared. The scouts fled back to the main party; the Indians did not pursue them.

The white men were in a dangerous spot with a bluff on one side, a cliff behind them, and a deep river all along their route. They had ridden right into a trap laid by Numaga. When the time was right, Numaga gave the signal and allowed one hundred warriors to show themselves to the whites. One Indian rode forward with what looked like a battle ax. When he saw him, Captain McDonald ordered the men to fire at the Indian. The Indian retreated, but as soon as he reached the main body of warriors, all the warriors started riding toward the white men.

Suddenly, confronting the Indians didn't seem like such a good idea to McDonald. He wanted to retreat to a grove of cottonwoods so they would at least have some cover, but Ormsby was rallying the men. He and thirty or forty others charged up a slope toward the approaching Indians. As soon as they got to the top of the ridge, rifle fire opened up all around them. Some white men lost their weapons when their frightened horses bucked. Those who still had their guns couldn't see who to shoot at because the late afternoon sun was in their eyes.

Ormsby spotted some Indians circling around to cut off the white men's line of retreat. He immediately gave the order to fall back and regroup. Ormsby reached a gulch near the cottonwoods where he thought the white men could make a stand. But the Indians followed and attacked. The white men held them off for about ten minutes, but the Indians had long-range rifles, while most of the white men had only revolvers and pistols. Soon the Paiutes were shooting at the white men from the cottonwood grove. The Indians had them surrounded. The volunteers tried to run out of the gulch toward the mouth of the Truckee. Some tried to escape by crossing the river, but it was too high and flowing too fast from spring runoff. They were pushed back to shore by the current where the Indians could shoot at them.

Numaga could see the whites were defeated. He wasn't interested in seeing senseless slaughter, especially of men that he generally got along with. He tried to call off his warriors. But one of his subchiefs, Sequinata, would not listen. His band pursued the whites, and momentum carried the rest of the Indians in pursuit.

Some white men, led by Condon and Watkins, managed to get up a steep, slippery path and escape to the plateau. Numaga again tried to call off his warriors and again they ignored him. They were too carried away with getting their revenge on the whites. The white men were too tired, too poorly equipped, and too unorganized to put up a defense. Ormsby and somewhere between forty-five and seventy other white men were killed.

It started to get dark and some whites took refuge in the shadows. They waited in their hiding places for hours, until the Indians had left. It was midnight before they finally came out of hiding and made their way to Buckland's Station. A new force of seven hundred volunteers and soldiers went after the Paiutes on June 3. Though they engaged the Paiutes in battle, the Indians put up such a clever and strong defense that most of them escaped. The next day, an army detachment pursued the Paiutes to Pyramid Lake, but when they arrived, the Paiutes had left their village.

Afterward, Colonel Frederick W. Lander and some Paiute chiefs sat down to negotiate a new peace. The Paiutes retained 500,000 acres of their original territory around Pyramid Lake as their reservation, though it wasn't made official until March 23, 1874. The long delay in officially creating the reservation allowed white settlers to establish homesteads in Paiute territory. They were allowed to stay, but only after paying the Paiutes for title to the land.

The Fastest Ride
· 1860 ·

In the spring of 1860, Bolivar Roberts hired about fifty young men to work for the Pony Express, a horse-and-man-powered mail delivery route between St. Joseph, Missouri, and Sacramento, California. Most of the men he chose were young, wiry, unmarried, and many of them were experienced guides, scouts, and couriers. One of those men was Robert "Pony Bob" Haslam.

On May 9, 1860, Haslam got ready for his regular ride from Friday's Station to Buckland's Station, seventy-five miles to the east. He checked his Spencer rifle and Colt revolver and saddled up his horse, probably a half-breed California mustang. This was the type of horse the company usually picked, and Haslam liked them especially wild. Over his saddle he swung the mochila, a leather tote specially designed to fit like a blanket over the saddle. The mochila had four pouches, two of which rested on each side of the horse. The rider's legs rested between each pair of pouches on either side of the horse. Oilskin-wrapped mail was secured inside the pouches, which were locked at the beginning of the mochila's journey. There was usually no more than twenty pounds of mail.

When Haslam left Friday's Station at the south end of Lake Tahoe, he probably didn't know that an Indian war had broken out to the north. He changed horses at a town called Genoa. Then he rode at his regular pace for another ten or twelve miles to the relay station at Carson City, where he expected to get a new horse and ride on. But as soon as he arrived, he knew something was amiss. There were no fresh horses. He didn't know it, but they had been taken for the volunteers who had ridden after the Paiutes.

He had no choice but to go on. So he rested a bit, fed his horse, and continued on to Reed's Station, but there were no horses there either. He rested awhile and then rode on again. Now he was really worried about getting the mail through, so he rode a slightly different route than normal from Reed's Station to Buckland's Station. Along that run he was wounded twice by Indians, but he made it to Buckland's Station. When he arrived, Haslam expected to turn the mail over to the next rider. But that rider, Johnson Richardson, was so scared of the Indians that he refused to take the mail, so the stationmaster, W. C. Harley, offered Haslam fifty dollars to keep going east with the mail. He did it, not for the money, but for duty. Besides, "Pony Bob" was known to be one of the most fearless Pony Express riders and he had to live up to his reputation. He changed horses and rode on.

It was a hot, dusty, lonely, thirty-five-mile ride to Carson's Sink. Haslam rode thirty more miles from there, through alkali flats and sandy hills, before finally arriving at the Sand Springs station, where he changed horses. There was not a drop of water to be had along the way. He rode thirty-seven more miles to Cold Springs, where he changed horses again. Thirty miles later he finally arrived at Smith's Creek, after having ridden 190 miles without rest. There, rider Jay Kelley took the mochila from him.

After getting about eight hours sleep, Haslam got ready to take the westbound mail to Friday's Station. On his return trip, Haslam arrived at the Cold Springs station only to find it had been attacked by Indians. The station had been burned down, the keeper killed, and the horses run off. Haslam watered his horse and continued on his way. By the time he reached Sand Springs, it was starting to get dark. Some of the sagebrush was so tall that it could easily hide a horse, so Haslam kept a close lookout for Indians. He also watched his horse for signs that it detected other animals in the area. Fortunately, he reached Sand Springs unmolested. Haslam convinced the stationkeeper there to come with him, fearing that he would be killed if left alone. The stationkeeper agreed and went with Haslam. This may have saved the keeper's life, for Smith's Creek was attacked the next day and Sand Springs could have been next. When they reached Carson Sink, they found fifteen men barricaded in the station. They had recently seen fifty painted warriors ride by. The adobe station was large enough for the men and their horses to hide inside. Haslam left them as they were and continued riding. After dark, he finally reached Buckland's Station, only three and a half hours late.

Stationmaster Harley was so relieved to see that Haslam was still alive, he paid him twice the amount promised him. Haslam rested a short time before riding to Carson City, taking time to visit Bolivar Roberts before riding back to Friday's Station. When the trip came to an end, Haslam had ridden a total of 380 miles in just thirty-six hours!

The battles with the Paiutes continued to disrupt the Pony Express. The extraordinary feats of the riders were documented in the media, and Haslam, and others like him, were hailed as national heroes.

When the telegraph from the Missouri River to Sacramento was completed on October 24, 1861, the Pony Express was out of business. Wells Fargo continued to operate a pony express at its own expense between San Francisco and Virginia City, so Haslam rode his old route until the railroad was completed across the Sierra Nevada in 1869. He then transferred to the Wells Fargo operation between Virginia City and Reno. When the telegraph was completed between Virginia City and Reno, Haslam transferred to a pony express line in Montana. He even designed a business card that showed himself as a pony express rider.

To commemorate the heroism and uniqueness of the Pony Express, the Bureau of Land Management has marked the original route for travelers in Utah, Wyoming, and Nevada. In Nevada, the Pony Express route stretches 420 miles from Lake Tahoe to the Goshute Indian Reservation on the Utah border. Wooden signs mark important road intersections, and posts marked "XP" (the

Pony Express brand) line the route at mile intervals. Roadside displays featuring information on the Pony Express can be found in Churchill County in western Nevada and White Pine County in eastern Nevada.

The Battle of Egan Canyon
· 1860 ·

Howard Egan worked as the manager of the Salt Lake District of the Pony Express, which stretched from Salt Lake City to Robert's Creek, three hundred miles away in Nevada. Egan established the stations on his route, delivered supplies, and hired stationmasters and men to tend the livestock. More than once Egan himself rode parts of the route.

Once Egan rode the route for a sick rider. As he approached rocky, narrow Egan Canyon, he saw a fire up ahead, surrounded by Indians. He quickly had to decide what to do. He could backtrack north and travel through another canyon several miles away or he could ride straight through the camp. He decided to try the latter. He charged his horse through the camp, yelling loudly and firing his gun. The Indians scattered, afraid a large party of white men was about to attack. Egan's ruse worked. He got through the canyon safely.

The incident was a prelude of events to come. In May of 1860, a skirmish broke out between the Paiutes of northern Nevada and the white settlers in the area. Known as the Pyramid Lake War or the Paiute War, the disturbance caused major disruption of the Pony Express activities across Nevada.

One October day, stationmaster Mike Holton and Slim Wilson, the eastbound rider on his way to Schell Creek, were sitting down to breakfast at the Egan Canyon station. To their surprise, a party of about eighty Indians suddenly surrounded the station. They were dressed for war in loincloths and paint. They waved their tomahawks and yelled loudly. Holton stuck his head out the door and tried to talk peace with them, but he was rewarded for his effort by an arrow shot into the cabin wall next to his head. He ducked back inside and with the help of Wilson, filled sacks of grain to barricade the door and window.

The two men tried to out-shoot the Indians but didn't do much damage to the enemy force. They continued firing until they were nearly out of ammunition. They decided to make the last rounds count, so they tried to storm out the door, firing their guns. The chief stepped in and stopped the fight, demanding that the white men give the Indians food. The men immediately complied, handing out all the bacon, sugar, and bread they had on hand. But it wasn't enough. The chief demanded that the men start a fire and bake more bread while they waited. So the men did. The Indians taunted them the entire time they cooked. The chief sat calmly at the kitchen table, smoking tobacco and talking.

Meanwhile, Pony Express Rider Billy Dennis, arriving from the west with his delivery, saw the Indians surrounding the station. Before the Indians could spot him, he turned around and rode hard for help. He had passed a company of cavalry a few miles back, on their way to Salt Lake City. He told the soldiers what he had seen. The officer in charge, a Lieutenant Weed, sent twenty men ahead to cut off the entrance to the canyon. He took sixty more men directly to the station.

His timing was perfect. The two men holed up in the station had baked their last loaf of bread, and the chief had just informed the men that he intended to kill them at sundown. The Indians ripped blankets into strips then dragged the two white men outside and tied them to a wagon tongue with the strips. The Indians piled up sagebrush all around their captives and lit the pile on fire. They were whooping and yelling and dancing in circles when the cavalry rode in at sunset. The Indians scattered just as the flames were reaching the captives' boots.

A battle ensued. The two men were immediately rescued and

given rifles to join in the fight. The firepower of the well-armed cavalry was overwhelming. In a very short time, eighteen Indians, including the chief, were killed and many others were wounded. The Indians recognized a superior force and ran away before worse damage could be done. The white men captured about sixty Indian ponies. Only three soldiers were killed and several others were wounded.

Even after this overwhelming defeat, the Indians did not stay away from Egan Canyon. Just after the battle at Egan Canyon Station, two Pony Express riders, Thomas Dobson and James Cumbo, were riding through the canyon when they were discovered by Indians. Luckily the Indians did not have firearms, though several arrows came very close to the fleeing white men. After being pursued for about twenty miles, the men were finally able to escape into the darkness. Indians continued to raid Egan Canyon so frequently that a company of cavalry was assigned to protect the route.

A Famous Sack
of Flour
· 1864 ·

The Civil War was still at its height when Austin, Nevada, held its first election. As with many other states and territories in the West, Nevada had supporters for both the North and the South. During Austin's election for mayor, supporters for both sides nominated a candidate. The Confederates (Democrats) supported David E. Buel, a man known and respected by the local miners. Union supporters (Republicans) favored a young man named Charles Holbrook, who owned one of the newest stores in town.

The night before the election, the local brass band led a torch-lit parade down Main Street. Men placed bets on the outcome of the vote. One of the bets on the mayoral race was placed by R. C. Gridley. Mr. Gridley bet his friend, Dr. Henry S. Herrick, that his candidate, Buel, would beat Holbrook, Dr. Herrick's favorite. If Herrick lost, he would carry a fifty-pound sack of flour up Main Street from the First Ward to the Fourth Ward, a distance of about one and a quarter miles, marching to the tune of "Dixie." If Gridley lost, he would carry the flour the same distance marching to the tune of "Old John Brown."

Holbrook won by a narrow margin. The collection of the bet by Herrick on April 20 was quite an affair. At ten o'clock in the morning, a large crowd and the town band assembled at Gridley's grocery store. A parade featuring the sack of flour soon got underway. Gridley carried the colorfully decorated flour sack up the street, led by mounted city officials and followed by Dr.

Herrick, his son, and members of the Democratic Central Committee. The town band followed along behind the committee. Many people marched along behind the band while others lined both sides of the street waving and cheering.

After the march was over, everyone gathered in the Bank Exchange saloon where the principals attended a ceremony for the delivery of the flour. Gridley, Herrick, and others gave speeches. After drinks all around, Gridley mounted his horse, which had been decorated with flags, and led the procession back to where the march had begun and everyone imbibed at the Grimes & Gibson saloon. Gridley placed the flour on a special stand, and auctioneer T.B. Wade took bids on the flour. Gridley started the bidding at $200. After several bids, the flour sold for $350. All the money went to the Sanitary Fund, a forerunner of the American Red Cross.

The reason for all this was that, after the election, the editor of the *Reese River Reveille* had sarcastically remarked that everyone had put all their money into betting rather than into making a charitable donation. It was the fourth time the editor had mentioned the Sanitary Fund, which was in the middle of a nationwide drive to collect money for the Civil War's wounded soldiers. But only a measly sixty dollars had been donated by the people of Austin.

Gridley made up for the deficit when he started the bidding on the sack of flour. Not only was $350 raised in the first round of bidding, but the flour was auctioned off several more times that day. The rivalry to outbid one another was intense. When the sale finally ended late that night, $4,021 had been collected for the Sanitary Fund. The next day the sale continued. The total reached $4,349.75. A San Francisco artist took photographs of Gridley and the sack of flour and sold them, contributing another $950.

News of the auction quickly spread. Gridley received requests from all over the state to bring his famous flour sack to other towns to auction it off again. He spent the next several months touring around the state with his flour sack. He first went to Virginia City, where he raised over $13,000! Silver City contributed $895. Dayton sold the sack for $1,299. Gold Hill anted up almost $7,000.

Gridley traveled west to San Francisco, where citizens auctioned off the flour again. From there he sailed to the Atlantic coast. Then he visited several other cities, ending at St. Louis, where the flour was auctioned off at the Sanitary Fund's fair in July of 1864. From there Gridley returned overland to Austin. It is not known exactly how much total money was raised but estimates range from $100,000 to $275,000.

Gridley did much to help the cause. Unfortunately, he put himself deeply into debt. When he returned home from his trip, his store was bordering on bankruptcy and his partners had left town. Austin citizens donated almost seven hundred dollars to help with his expenses, but he remained in Austin only another year before moving to California, where the weather was more favorable for his failing health. He died on November 24, 1870.

To permanently commemorate the famous sack of flour, the town adopted a city seal. The coat of arms on the seal consisted of a sack of flour with the motto "Sanitary Fund $5,000." The seal was surrounded by a wreath and the words "Common Council, City of Austin—Incorporated February 20, 1864." The seal was used until the mid-1870s, when the town was unincorporated. The famous flour sack is on permanent display at the Nevada Historical Society in Reno.

Mark Twain Finds Trouble in Virginia City
· 1864 ·

When Mark Twain came to Nevada in 1861, he was still known as Sam Clemens. Restless to try something new, he joined his brother Orion, who had been appointed the secretary of Nevada Territory, and made a few dollars a day working as his brother's clerk. He also worked in the lumber business, though he ended up broke. He tried prospecting but didn't find anything substantial. During this time, he periodically sent letters to the editors of various western papers. One of those papers was the *Territorial Enterprise* of Virginia City, Nevada.

His first submission to the *Territorial Enterprise* immediately caught Editor Goodman's attention. It was a tongue-in-cheek essay called "Professor Personal Pronoun" that poked fun at George Turner, chief justice of the Nevada Territory. Twain wrote the article as if Turner were talking. The article stopped in mid-sentence, and at the end there was an editor's note that stated the story couldn't be finished because the typesetter had run out of capital I's. And so began Mark Twain's illustrious career.

Twain was hired as the paper's city editor for twenty-five dollars a week. He also received bribes from restaurants and businesses that paid him for giving them favorable reviews in the paper. He wrote about inquests, court news, and mining news. On slow news days, Twain made up news. He once said: "Get your facts first, and then you can distort them as much as you please." He attacked the telegraph monopoly and prosecuting attorneys. He criticized the Carson City undertaker for charging astronomical prices. He poked fun at fellow reporters, society parties, the territorial legislature, and the constitutional conventions. He began using the name Mark Twain on February 2, 1863, when reporting on the constitutional convention at Carson City.

Fellow editor Dan DeQuille had used hoaxes to fill column space when news was slow, so the precedent was set for Mark Twain. One of his first hoaxes was a piece titled "The Petrified Man." He chose the topic because many people were interested in petrification at the time, and he thought it a bit ridiculous. He also had had a disagreement with the town's coroner so he thought he would poke fun at both at the same time. His story claimed that a petrified man had been found at Gravelly Ford near Winnemucca. The man looked about one hundred years old. An inquest was held and cause of death was judged to be protracted exposure.

Twain was stunned when everyone seemed to believe the story. But he was very satisfied when the story was reprinted around the country. He got a charge out of sending extra copies to the coroner, then sending miners over to the man's house to ask for extra copies of the story.

The beginning of the end of Mark Twain's stay in Virginia City began with a hoax called "The Latest Sensation." He wrote about a family named Hopkins that lived near Empire City. Mrs. Hopkins felt she was in danger because her husband had become violent. One day, Mr. Hopkins rode into town all cut up and with a scalp in his hand—it was Mrs. Hopkins' hair. The sheriff immediately rode out to the Hopkins house and found that seven of the nine Hopkins children had been killed. Furniture and clothing were strewn all around the rooms. Incredibly, Mrs. Hopkins was still alive. She later entered a hospital where she had a hairpiece made from her own hair. She died shortly afterwards of insanity. Mr. Hopkins had never been known to be violent but had been having financial difficulties that supposedly triggered his killing spree.

Readers were shocked. Twain wondered at their reaction. The story was meant to point out the dangers of stock manipulation, in which the fictional Hopkins had been engaged. Twain was amazed that the readers didn't even pick up on the fact that a mansion and a forest near Empire City such as he had described didn't even exist.

Other papers picked up the story. The *Gold Hill News* and the *San Francisco Bulletin* were outraged when they learned it was a hoax. The *News* editor felt Twain had smeared the reputation of the *Territorial Enterprise* by writing the story. The San Francisco paper demanded that Twain be fired. The editor of the *Reese River Reveille* in Austin was one man who wasn't taken in by Twain's story. About Twain he wrote that "we would not be surprised at anything done by that silly idiot." Many people canceled their subscriptions to the *Territorial Enterprise* and picked up the rival paper, the *Union*. Twain was depressed over the controversy, and he threatened to quit. Goodman convinced him to remain, but Twain's continued employment was now precarious.

The final blow came in May 1864 when Twain wrote an article called the "Grand Ball at Los Angeles Plata." He reported that some Carson City ladies had organized a ball, supposedly to raise money for the Union cause. He wrote that the money raised would instead be donated to a "Miscegenation Society" in the East, an organization, if such a thing existed, that advocated interracial marriages.

There was an element of truth to the article—several ladies in Carson City had in fact organized a ball as a fundraiser. In actuality the money was being raised for the Sanitary Commission, or Sanitary Fund. These ladies were outraged by the false story and wrote a letter of protest. The *Territorial Enterprise* would not publish it, but the *Union* did. The two papers had been competing to see which would contribute the most to the Sanitary Commission. Twain accused the *Union* of backing out on their pledges.

The Union responded with counter threats and accusations.

The argument reached such a pitch that Twain, encouraged by other members of the paper, challenged Laird, editor of the *Union*, to a duel. Twain and his seconds, Steve Gillis and Rollin Daggett, rode to a nearby ravine for the duel. Gillis was an expert marksman and had just shot the head off a bird about thirty paces away, when Laird and his seconds rode up. Gillis quickly pressed the gun into Twain's hand, congratulating him on his good shooting. Laird and his seconds hurriedly left town.

The news of the planned duel reached Carson City and a warrant was sworn out for Twain's arrest since dueling was illegal. But one of Twain's friendships of the past bore fruit. Governor James Nye warned Twain that he was about to be arrested. He gave him twenty-four hours to get out of town. Twain left immediately, only a few dollars richer than when he had arrived. A few years later, he wrote *Roughing It*, which chronicled his years in Nevada and California. He had worked a total of twenty months for the *Territorial Enterprise*, which launched a long literary career.

Fire Consumes the Yellow Jacket Mine
· 1869 ·

The Comstock Lode was a huge geological formation of ore that many mines, including the Yellow Jacket, Ophir, Empire, and Mexican, tapped. Peter O'Riley and Pat McLaughlin discovered the lode around June 1, 1859. They were working a claim along Six Mile Canyon and were just about to give up when they struck a rich deposit of silver. Thousands of prospectors were mining the Comstock within a matter of months.

Unlike the easy placer mining in California, the Comstock Lode was hard to reach. It was deep under the ground at Mount Davidson. Deep shafts and tunnels had to be blasted through solid rock to get to it. Cave-ins were common and so were fires. The first and most terrible fire at the Comstock Lode occurred at the Yellow Jacket Mine. Fire broke out about seven o'clock in the morning of Wednesday, April 7, 1869.

The fire started eight hundred feet below the surface of the earth, two hundred feet from the main shaft. Timbers used to shore up the mine shaft caught fire when someone from the night shift left a candle burning. At least three hours lapsed between the end of the night shift and the beginning of the day shift when the fire was discovered. Many of the workers on the day shift had already been lowered into the mines. Forty-five men had gone below in the Crown Point shaft alone.

Someone rang the fire alarm and firemen from nearby Gold Hill and Virginia City immediately responded. Engines from

Liberty Engine Co. No. 1, Yellow Jacket Engine Co. No. 2, and Nevada Hook & Ladder Company No. 1 arrived to fight the fire. Workers at the site worked frantically to get the miners out of the burning shafts. At first the smoke was so dense no one dared go into the mine for fear they would suffocate. Around nine o'clock, the smoke partially cleared away from the Kentuck shaft, so the men took a chance and descended into that shaft. They found the first two bodies at the bottom of the elevator. About noon, some firemen rode the elevator to the bottom of the Yellow Jacket Mine where they found three or four more dead men. Their bodies were placed in the elevators for their final ride to the top.

As soon as word of the fire spread to town, the families of the day-shift miners raced to the mine, hoping it wasn't their husband, brother, or uncle that was trapped beneath the surface. Reverend Patrick Manogue, known as the "giant priest" of St. Mary's in the Mountains, circulated among the families, offering what comfort he could. Some women insisted on seeing their loved ones one last time and were horrified at the destruction. Some bodies were damaged so badly by the fire that they were kept from view of their families.

Firemen worked quickly, trying to put the fire out with a very long hose. Miners cleared the way so that the firemen could pass on through the various shafts. Some of the tunnel walls were so hot that the men had to douse them with water before they could continue. In some areas, boiling water two or three inches deep pooled on the floor. The steam, sulfur fumes, and gases from the heated ore were so noxious that an air pipe from the main blower had to be routed from the surface so the men could continue fighting the fire.

The fire was still rising in intensity at nine o'clock that night. The blaze was fanned by the interconnecting ventilation drifts inside the three mine shafts. Smoke and fire spread from the Yellow Jacket into the Kentuck and Crown Point shafts. Firemen threaded a second water line down to the seven-hundred-foot level to combat the flames.

By two o'clock the next morning, thirteen bodies had been recovered. By one o'clock that afternoon, twenty-three bodies had been found. Some were thought to have been killed by an explosion near the Crown Point shaft, caused by noxious gases. At the nine-hundred-foot level, about thirty feet from the Crown Point shaft, nine men were found dead from asphyxiation.

On the morning of April 10, the fire had increased to such an extent that firemen couldn't risk trying to recover any more bodies or fight the fire. They closed the mouths of all the shafts, hoping to snuff out the fire. They also pumped steam from the boilers down the air shaft. On April 12, the firemen opened up the shafts temporarily and recovered a few more bodies. But the fire was still burning so fiercely that they quickly closed the mine again and continued pumping in steam.

On April 14, at three o'clock in the afternoon, the steam was shut off and all efforts were stopped. Five bodies were still unaccounted for. The mine was later reopened and the firemen conducted another search. Small fires were still burning as they wound their way through the mine. Some of the rescuers nearly suffocated and had to be rushed to the surface. On April 28, one of the five missing bodies was found, but by that time, all the firemen were suffering from oxygen deprivation and had to return to the surface.

Firemen continued to fight the fire until May 2, when the flames suddenly rose higher. They sealed the drifts between the Yellow Jacket and the Kentuck and Crown Point mines. Then they sealed the shafts, hoping to snuff the fire out. On May 18, they reopened the Kentuck and Crown Point shafts to continue looking for the last missing men. Two days later they found another body in the Crown Point shaft at the one-thousand-foot level. Shortly after that, the fire somehow fanned itself again, and it became too dangerous to continue the search. On May 24, firemen were finally able to confine the fire to one small area at the eight-hundred-foot level where it continued to burn for over a year! Three years after the fire, some rocks were still red hot. A few skeletal remains of the three men still missing were finally found in the area where the fire had been confined.

A total of forty-five men died in the fire. A mass funeral was held to mourn all of the victims. The funeral was one of the most extensive ever held at Virginia City or Gold Hill. A long line of mourners followed the bodies to Virginia City and Gold Hill cemeteries. Military and fire companies wore full dress uniforms.

Train Robbed Twice
in the Same Day
• 1870 •

Trains chugged along the transcontinental railroad for a year and a half before a single robbery occurred. The tiny town of Verdi, Nevada, would go down in history as the site of the first train robbery in the Far West. Even more incredible, the same train, the Central Pacific's Express Train No. 1, was robbed twice on the same day!

A. J. "Big Jack" Davis planned to rob the Central Pacific train on its regular run from San Francisco to the East Coast. To assist him, he hired six other nefarious characters including John Squires, an experienced stage robber, and Ed Parsons, a Virginia City gambler. Rounding out the group were Bill Cockrell, Sol Jones, Henry Gilchrist, and John Chapman.

Davis sent John Chapman to San Francisco to learn the schedule of the trains leaving for Nevada. Chapman learned that the next train would leave Oakland for the Sierras in the early morning of November 4, 1870. Chapman telegraphed Sol Jones, informing him of the schedule. It was perfect timing, since that train carried twenty-dollar gold pieces for the Yellow Jacket Mine payroll, plus bank notes and silver dollars. The total value was close to fifty thousand dollars.

Jones got the message to Davis, who was hiding out in an abandoned mine tunnel in the Peavine Mountains. From this vantage point, he could see the Central Pacific tracks. Two hours before the scheduled arrival of the train, he and the other men left the cave and rode to an old stone quarry six or seven miles from Verdi. Jones stayed with the horses at the quarry while the others rode into town. The men planned to board the train near the depot and ride it to the quarry. But the train was late. It had been delayed near Cisco, California, by a westbound freight train that had jumped the tracks.

When the train finally arrived, Davis and the others, armed with six-shooters and shotguns, jumped on the train and confronted conductor Frank Mitchell and forced him from the engine into another train car. The robbers ordered the passengers to lie down on the floor of one of the passenger cars. Then one of the robbers uncoupled the engine and express car from the rest of the train, leaving the passenger cars behind. Davis ordered the engineer, Henry Small, to drive the train a short distance down the track, where Jones waited with the horses. Davis and his men busted open the express car, broke into the treasure chest, and loaded about forty-one thousand dollars in gold coins and bars into sacks. No one was hurt during the holdup.

Ten hours later, at Independence Station, near Elko, Nevada, the same train, now back intact, was robbed again. The train had stopped at Independence to replenish its water supply. Fortunately, a man named Marshall, the Wells Fargo agent on board, heard the bandits coming and hid most of the remaining gold. When he opened the safe for the thieves, it contained only about $3,100 that the first robbers had overlooked. The thieves took it.

Neither set of crooks got away with their crimes for very long. Just after the first robbery, the railroad cars that had been uncoupled from the train coasted down an incline until they bumped into the engine. The crew coupled the train back together and steamed to Reno to alert the sheriff. Wells Fargo and the Central Pacific Railroad officials immediately posted rewards of forty thousand dollars for the crooks. Law officers from all over California and Nevada rode to Virginia City to aid in the search. Washoe County Sheriff Calvin Pegg and Undersheriff James H. Kinkead organized a posse to pursue the robbers. Wells Fargo detectives from San Francisco, including F. T. Burke, joined the hunt.

The night of the robberies John Squires, Ed Parsons, and James Gilchrist checked into Pearson's Tavern in Sardine Valley, California. Mrs. Pearson noticed their suspicious behavior and their twenty-dollar gold pieces, and she summoned the local sheriff, who organized a posse that soon captured Gilchrist. From information given by Gilchrist, Undersheriff Kinkead captured Parsons and Squires in California.

Meanwhile, Wells Fargo Detective Burke observed Sol Jones spending a large amount of gold around town. After Burke pressured him, Jones admitted he was involved in the robbery. He told Burke all about the plot and gave him the names of the others. His information led to the capture of Cockrell in a saloon near Reno. Chapman was captured at the Reno depot when he got off the train from San Francisco. Since all the men were still carrying some of the gold they had stolen when they were captured and they confessed to the location of the rest, nearly all of the money was recovered.

The men were quickly tried in a packed Washoe City courtroom. Townspeople were amazed that Davis was involved since he was a respected Virginia City businessman. Few of the townspeople knew of his criminal past. On Christmas Eve, four of the men were sentenced from eighteen to twenty-two years in the state prison. Squires was sentenced to twenty years in prison because of his prior robberies. Parsons was also sentenced to twenty years in prison because of his past gambling activities. Cockrell, also a known road agent, received twenty-two years hard labor for his role in the robbery. Chapman, a one-time Sunday School superintendent received eighteen years. Jones received a sentence of only five years because he cooperated with the law. Gilchrist went free for testifying against the others. In September 1871, Cockerell, Chapman, Parsons, and Squires led a violent prison break. Eventually they all were recaptured. Parsons was pardoned in November 1881.

At the trial, Davis claimed that he had been forced to become a train robber because Wells Fargo had taken such means to protect its stages. This forced him into a new line of work! He must have won some sympathy with the jury since he got only ten years prison time. The governor reduced his sentence to three years and set him free after two years. He may have received his freedom só early as a result of helping save some guards from being killed in an 1871 prison riot.

Unfortunately, Davis did not learn his lesson. He immediately planned a stage robbery. His life of crime ended on September 3, 1875, when he was killed by Wells Fargo Agent Eugene Blair while attempting to rob the Eureka-to-Tybo stage at Willow Station.

Wells Fargo offered a reward of five thousand dollars for the arrest of the men who had robbed the train at Independence. A posse made up of men from the Central Pacific Railroad, soldiers from nearby Fort Halleck, and officers from the Elko sheriff's department chased the robbers across the desert near the Ruby Mountains, following a trail of gold and silver coins that had spilled from the robbers' saddlebags.

Along the trail, the pursuers found a glove with the name Edward Carr on it. They also found a brass locket with the name and company of a soldier named Harvey. This was enough evidence to prove that the robbers were deserters from Fort Halleck. The men were captured then convicted on January 13, 1871, and sentenced to ten years of hard labor. Wells Fargo recovered all of the money stolen in the latter robbery.

Raymond and Ely Thwart Claim Jumpers
· 1870 ·

Though it didn't have the reputation of Tombstone, Arizona, or Dodge City, Kansas; Pioche, Nevada, was quite a rowdy town in its heyday. As was typical of many mining towns, the big boom Pioche experienced attracted thieves, gamblers, outlaws, and soiled doves to town. Many of the first people buried in the local cemetery died a violent death.

In 1870 Pioche was home to two major mining companies. The Raymond and Ely Mine, owned by William H. Raymond and John H. Ely, was one of the earliest silver mines in the district. They had purchased the property from Ed and Patrick Burke in 1869. They also purchased several lots around the mine to protect their find.

The other major claim, located on the other side of the mountain from Raymond and Ely's mine, was owned by brothers Tom and Frank Newlands. They were having difficulty reaching the vein of ore, so they needed to dig a tunnel in order to approach their vein from another angle. The Washington and Creole Mine, also owned by Raymond and Ely, stood in their way. But Raymond and Ely figured the Washington and Creole Mine was probably worthless, so they allowed the Newlands to dig through their property.

But instead of finding a minor vein in the Washington and Creole Mine, the Newlands discovered very rich ore. Their discovery was assayed at about three hundred dollars a ton. The brothers asked Raymond and Ely for an additional thirty days to mine the find. The mine owners granted their request, but when the thirty days were up, the Newlands would not leave. Raymond and Ely ordered the brothers to get off their property. The Newlands brothers refused, barricaded themselves in the tunnel, and continued to mine the claim.

This was enough for Raymond and Ely. They hired four outlaws—Morgan Courtney, Michael Casey, Barney Flood, and William Bethers—to take back their property in exchange for about twenty dollars a day. In addition, Courtney also a extracted a promise from Raymond and Ely to allow the outlaws to work the claim for thirty days after they won it back.

Courtney spent some time watching the routine of the men who worked for the Newlands brothers. He noted their starting and quitting times. He noted the number of men and the types of jobs they had. Most importantly, he noticed that several times a day supplies were hauled to the camp by horse-drawn wagon. It was a weak spot that could be exploited. The Newlands brothers had also hired some gunmen, and Courtney watched their habits as well.

Courtney bribed one of the men who regularly transported supplies to the Newlands camp. For his money, Courtney got a keg of whiskey delivered to the Newlands workers. Courtney figured that the men would freely imbibe, leaving them vulnerable.

That night, November 9, 1870, while the miners drank themselves into a stupor, Raymond and Ely's outlaws hid behind some pine trees near the mouth of the tunnel. When the time was right, Courtney led the charge into the crowd. The outlaws fired their pistols and chased the men away from the mine. Before the smoke cleared, one man was dead and several others were wounded.

Courtney and his band had won back Raymond and Ely's property. Raymond and Ely paid the money that they owed the outlaws and followed through on their promise to allow the outlaws to mine the property for thirty days. The men made sixty thousand dollars in those thirty days, selling the ore back to Raymond and Ely.

A month later, Courtney was charged with killing W. G. Snell, the Newlands worker who had died in the shootout. But when Raymond, considered one of the most respectable men in town, posted Courtney's bail, the charge was dropped. Courtney met his end in 1873, when he was shot several times by James McKinney in a dispute over a woman. Michael Casey was killed in a gunfight shortly after mining the Raymond and Ely property. Barney Flood left the area after knifing a man. William Bethers also left town and was later killed, apparently at Eureka, Nevada.

Raymond and Ely were criticized for hiring gunmen to settle their differences with the Newlands instead of letting the law handle it, but the furor over the incident quickly died down. From 1870 to 1873, they extracted over forty million dollars worth of silver from the Washington and Creole Mine. It was one of the most prosperous mines in eastern Nevada.

The Sazerac
Lying Club
· 1877 ·

Austin was one of many towns in Nevada that rose to life during a silver strike. William Talcott discovered silver in Pony Canyon on May 2, 1862. The following January, word about the silver strike spread, and the stampede to the Reese River Mining District began. Austin was built on a hill close to the mines.

The town boomed for several years. There were less than fifty buildings in late May 1863, but just three months later there were 279! Though the town had its share of rowdies, overall it was quite civilized. Almost from the start, Austin had a church, school, and various fraternal organizations. Its pride and joy was its famous newspaper, the *Reese River Reveille*.

William C. Phillips started publishing the *Reese River Reveille* on May 16, 1863. It was a small four-page weekly when it first began; at peak times it was published daily. At one time, Myron Angel, who later became a well-known Nevada historian, worked as an assistant to the editor. The paper was widely read right from the start, but it gained real notoriety during the tenure of Editor Fred G. Hart.

Hart was the editor from 1873 to 1878. His main job was to collect local news stories, but sometimes it was difficult to find material to fill the pages. One day, on his way home from work, he stopped at the Sazerac, a local saloon named for a popular kind of brandy. Hart listened to the men around him, hoping to pick up some tidbit for the newspaper. This particular day, he heard a man bragging about seeing a huge stack of silver bars waiting shipment in Mexico. He said the stack of silver was seven miles long, forty feet high, and thirteen feet wide. Hart knew this was an exaggeration because even the famous Comstock Lode, the largest silver strike ever, did not produce that much.

He thought nothing more of the story until the next day when he was assembling the next edition of the paper. There was very little news to report. Remembering the man's story from the previous night, he was inspired. If he couldn't find any real news, he would make some up. He took a cue from the braggart. On the spot, he created the Sazerac Lying Club, reporting:

> The Sazerac Lying Club was organized last night, our esteemed, prominent and respected fellow citizen, Mr. George Washington Fibley, being unanimously chosen president of the organization. There was no opposing candidate; his claims and entire fitness for the honorable position being conceded by common consent of the club.

Hart identified the members of the fictitious club using various aliases. He stated that the club was restricted to men only and membership was tightly controlled. Ladies would be allowed in the saloon but could not participate in club meetings. Hart also wrote that "Article one hundred and nineteen of our constitution and bylaws expressly forbids and prohibits the admission of professional liars into this here club . . . reporters, politicians, and others as lie for money, included."

Most citizens found the article amusing, though the man who recognized himself as the fictitious Fibley demanded an apology. Hart apologized the next day by stating that Fibley had actually been defeated in the election for president.

Hart then reported on club "meetings." He had worked in many mining communities in Nevada and California, so he had plenty of material on which to base his make-believe Lying Club characters. One such liar was "Uncle John" Gibbons, a stage driver. One day Gibbons told the Lying Club why the stage was late. He claimed he was delayed by a large flock of sage hens blocking the road. He had to unhitch the lead horse and ride back to the stage station for help. By the time he returned with two men, the birds were gone. The delay had caused the stage to arrive late.

Hart also invented a character named "Old Dad." One day Old Dad explained why the telegraph that reached from Austin to Salt Lake City went down. The line was called a "quadraplex" system, which meant that four messages could be sent at one time over the same wire. Old Dad said he saw the wire sagging and straining at the weight of the words. Words were dropping off the wire in chunks because there were so many. The wire had a knot in it, so he figured the words were getting backed up behind it. He tried to straighten the wire out, but just then a story about a war between the Turks and the Russians came through and knocked him down, so he dropped the wire like a hot potato. He proceeded into town to report the difficulties to the telegraph office. He told the operator that he had sent a man to the site of the knot with a crowbar to "pry out some of the biggest words and smooth the knot down, so the words could pass each other."

One edition of the paper carried a story about how the liars tested their bylaws regarding membership. They were trying to decide if a newspaper editor from San Francisco should be allowed to join the club. Some argued that editors couldn't lie; therefore, he shouldn't be allowed in the club. But one man furnished evidence that the man could lie. He had read a story written by the man in question in which a woman stepped on a needle that embedded in her foot. Many years later when her children had children, the needle reappeared in the grandchild, poking from the grandchild's head. "Now if that ain't a lie, I'd like to know what you call it," said the witness. The president of the Lying Club ruled on the decision, voting against admission because the man was obviously a professional liar!

The chronicles of the Sazerac Lying Club were reprinted in

other regional and national newspapers. Even a German paper picked up the stories. A San Francisco publishing firm asked Hart to collect the stories to be published in a book, which he did. He wrote an introduction to the book that warned booksellers not to give any refunds to buyers claiming the book was a fraud.

On November 20, 1877, Hart disbanded his fictitious Sazerac Lying Club. In his last article on the subject, Hart wrote an account of the last meeting of the club, in which the president called an end to the club. Hart wrote it as if he were the president of the club, asking permission from club members to use the club's "archives" for the book requested by the San Francisco firm.

Hart left Austin and in 1880 became the editor of the *Territorial Enterprise* at Virginia City. He abruptly left that newspaper after printing an inflammatory article about James D. Fair, a senatorial candidate, not realizing that Fair's partner, John McKay, was part owner of the paper. Hart later worked on San Francisco and Sacramento papers before dying on August 29, 1897.

Absalom Lehman
Discovers Cave
· 1885 ·

Absalom Lehman was one of many settlers who bought property in eastern Nevada in the mid-1800s. His ranch was situated along a creek that flowed off nearby Wheeler Peak. There was a strange depression on the property—this small hole piqued Lehman's curiosity. Lehman started digging around it and found that the hole grew much larger below the surface. When the hole was big enough to crawl through, he squirmed through it. His eyes widened at the delightful surprise below him. He had just discovered a world of beautiful stalactites and stalagmites! The cave system would later be named for him.

A humorous legend connected with the discovery of the cave claims that Lehman was exploring on horseback, when the horse suddenly broke through a weak spot in the cave's roof. Before plunging to the bottom, Lehman lassoed a tree and held on until he was rescued four days later. His legs were permanently disfigured from hanging onto the horse all that time!

How did Lehman come to be there? Absalom Lehman left Pennsylvania and traveled to California during the gold rush days, but he did not find much gold. He traveled to Australia to prospect, and there he married his first wife. After she died in 1861, he came back to the United States. He remarried in Denver. In 1869, he and his wife, Olive, moved to Nevada and built a ranch and planted an orchard. They sold food to nearby mining camps. Due to health problems, Olive had to leave the area in 1881, taking their two children with her. It was after he returned from visiting her that

Lehman was poking around on his property and made the great discovery. A candle lantern was his sole light source, but it was enough to illuminate the remarkable limestone cave.

Lehman probably did not realize that thousands of years of chemical reactions had formed the cave. If he had, he may have been able to help prevent later damage to the cave. The limestone beneath Wheeler Peak had been carved by ordinary water mixed with carbon dioxide, which dissolved the rock, leaving hollow spaces and scalloped walls. Later the water drained out of the cave, and then water began percolating into the cave from the surface. This water contained dissolved calcite, which created the various formations inside the cave.

Lehman may not have realized the scientific significance of what he had found, but he immediately recognized the moneymaking potential. He started charging people one dollar each to enter the cave. He did not take them through the cave, but he did give each person a candle and reassurance that someone would come looking for them if they got lost. Some areas of the cave could only be reached by crawling, but the sights were worth the inconvenience. People were dazzled by the unusual formations inside the cave.

The limestone cave was about a quarter of a mile long and was situated approximately 6,800 feet above sea level on the flank of Wheeler Peak. The familiar stalactites and stalagmites were everywhere. A unique formation, called a shield, was common in this cave. One fantastic shield, called the Parachute, has a generally round shape with stalactites hanging from it. Unfortunately, some of the formations were destroyed by early explorers who used sledgehammers to break trails through the cave. Further destruction was caused by people who used the cave as a ballroom. They destroyed a large formation to make room for a band to play. Some people used candles to burn their initials into the walls of the cave.

For awhile Lehman made quite a profit allowing people to visit the cave. He did so well that he decided to sell his ranch and live off the proceeds from the cave. But before the sale could go through, he died in Salt Lake City, on October 11, 1891.

The Rhodes family, nearby neighbors, bought the cave area from the estate and promoted the cave until 1922. That year, the government took control of the area and named it the Lehman Caves National Monument. In 1933, the caves became part of the National Park System. Archaeological digs in 1938 and in 1964 uncovered human bones that were much older than Lehman's era. Indians had probably lived there or used it for ceremonies.

When Great Basin National Park was established as America's forty-ninth national park on October 27, 1986, the Lehman Caves became part of the park. The main attraction today is the Gothic Palace, which is filled with columns, draperies, and stalactites. The Lake Room is also impressive with tranquil pools and "soda straws" which are hollow limestone tubes, through which water is still dripping. The Grand Palace contains shields, massive columns, and "bacon rind" draperies. The formations continue to grow at the rate of one inch every one hundred years. They will continue to grow as long as water continues to seep into the cave. If you look closely, you may also see cave dwellers such as pack rats and cave crickets.

Bank Robbery at Winnemucca
· 1900 ·

The heydays of the Wild West were coming to a close. Butch Cassidy and the Sundance Kid had had their fun, but it was time to pack it in. But before they gave up their outlaw ways, they had to pull one last job to finance their getaway to South America. They had robbed a train three weeks earlier in Tipton, Wyoming, but they had gotten very little from it. Bill Carver, a member of Butch and Sundance's Wild Bunch gang, went with them to pull another job at Winnemucca, Nevada.

Butch and Sundance camped for about ten days by the CS Ranch near Winnemucca. A boy named Vic Button and his friend Lee Case visited the outlaws daily, not realizing who they were. It was round-up time, so the outlaws just looked like another group of cowhands. Button lived at the CS Ranch. He was fascinated by a white horse the outlaws had and wanted to trade for it. He showed up every day with another horse, hoping to trade for the white horse. Butch took advantage of the boy's naivete and pumped him for information about Winnemucca.

On September 19, 1900, the three outlaws rode into town. The streets were crowded when they ducked inside a nearby saloon for a drink before robbing the bank. Then Butch and Sundance approached the bank and scouted around it, while Carver waited with a carbine rolled up in a blanket. Butch and Sundance signaled to Carver when they were ready.

When the three men walked into the First National Bank, three customers waited at the cashier's window. One outlaw held a gun on cashier McBride and demanded the cash from the vault. McBride tried to stall, telling them only the bank president, George Nixon, could open the vault. Nixon said the time lock was on and he could not open the door, but when a bandit held a knife to his throat, he opened the safe.

Once Nixon filled their bag with gold, the robbers led Nixon, McBride, a bookkeeper named Hill, a stenographer named Calhoun, and W. S. Johnson, a horse trader who happened to be conducting business in the bank, outside to the small yard behind the bank. Two robbers jumped over the back fence and retrieved their horses. Then the last robber followed them. As soon as they were out of sight, Nixon rushed back into the bank and grabbed his revolver. He fired several shots to alarm the townspeople.

Outside, the outlaws mounted up, fired their guns in the air, and rode away with $32,640. They had stolen $31,000 in twenty-dollar gold pieces, $1,200 in five- and ten-dollar coins, and the rest in bills.

When the robbers flew across Cross Creek Bridge, near the edge of town, the bag of gold slipped to the ground. They all halted while one robber quickly jumped off his horse, recovered the sack, and tossed it to another robber. Then they headed out of town at full tilt. Nixon and a customer rode after the bandits, firing away, but all of the shots missed. Attracted by the gunshots, Deputy Sheriff George Rose came running down the street. He commandeered a Southern Pacific locomotive to give chase. But the bandits soon outdistanced him.

The robbers raced out of town toward Golconda. After six miles, they mounted fresh horses that they had stolen that morning from Nixon. A few more miles out they changed horses again. About twenty miles from Winnemucca, the bandits changed horses at Clover Ranch.

A posse formed at Golconda, seventeen miles east of Winnemucca, to join in the chase. The group of men arrived at Clover Ranch just as the robbers were changing horses. One of the outlaws called out to the posse, "give the white horse to the kid on the CS Ranch," which the posse later did. Some of the ranch hands joined up with the posse and helped track the robbers north. But the robbers had relay points every ten miles or so, all the way to the Idaho border. The posse chased the robbers to Star Valley, Wyoming but never caught them. Finally, the posse had to turn back.

Nixon immediately questioned anyone who might have known anything about the gunmen. Telegraphs were sent to nearby towns such as Tuscarora. Physical descriptions were sent to lawmen around the West. At first a sheepshearer named Perkins was suspected since he disappeared right after the robbery. Three of his friends, Melville Fuller, Frances Silve, and Willie Wier, were also suspected. But everyone wanted to believe that Butch Cassidy and the Sundance Kid were the culprits.

The bank hired the Pinkerton Detective Agency to hunt for the robbers. About six weeks after the robbery, someone discovered the place where the bandits had camped. Torn up pieces of letters were found and sent to the Pinkertons, hoping to learn something about the robbers. One letter was addressed to a C. E. Rowe, who Nixon thought was the real bandit leader. The Pinkertons didn't catch up with the robbers, so the bank hired bounty hunter Tom Horn, the "enforcer" for the Wyoming Cattlemen's Association. Nixon offered a reward of one thousand dollars for each of the three bandits.

A few months later, the bank received a photo from New York City. The picture showed Butch, Sundance, and other members of the Wild Bunch dressed in business clothes. Fred Dodge, a Wells Fargo detective, had spotted the picture in a photo gallery while working undercover in Forth Worth, Texas, and forwarded it to the Pinkertons, who positively identified the men in the picture as Butch Cassidy and his gang. The agency sent the picture to Winnemucca to help in the search for the bank robbers. When Nixon saw the photo, he claimed that none of the men in the picture were the same as the men who had robbed the bank that day. This fact has led some people to believe that it was not

Butch and Sundance who robbed the Winnemucca bank in 1900. Another factor that has discounted Butch and Sundance as the culprits is the timing. Their last known holdup at Tipton, Wyoming, on August 29 was six hundred miles away. There wouln't hqave been enough time for Butch and Sundance to pull that job, travel to Winnemucca, and camp for ten days, in time to pull the bank job on September 19.

But the Pinkertons must have been convinced because they offered a six-thousand-dollar reward for the capture of Butch and Sundance in connection with the Winnemucca bank robbery. And later, when Butch and Sundance were killed in South America, the search for the Winnemucca bank robbers was terminated.

Butch and Sundance pulled off one more train robbery in the United States on July 3, 1901, in Wagner, Montana. They got away with sixty-five thousand dollars. After that the Wild Bunch disbanded and Butch and Sundance fled to South America. Though their deaths were widely reported in 1909, rumors persist to this day that Butch survived the shootout and lived until the 1930s. Though some people believe it was not them, Butch and Sundance are usually still given blame for the bank robbery at Winnemucca.

Labor Troubles at Ely
· 1903 ·

Trouble was brewing at the Martin Mine at Ely. Miners and mill workers felt they should be paid a better wage. They were only being paid three dollars per day while other mines in the district were paying three and a half dollars per day. The Martin Mine employees wanted at least the same amount that the other miners were making. The workers, led by union leader William Lloyd, decided to strike.

The mine's manager, John Traylor, quickly wrote a letter to the mine's owner, Mulford Martin, who lived in New York, advising him to pay the workers what they wanted so they could get the mine up and running again. He asked the miners to wait until he received a response from Martin.

But after just a short time, the men got impatient. They went to Traylor and told him to either meet their demands or leave town. Traylor felt threatened, so he visited the office of Judge Walker, the company's attorney. The two men arranged to meet Lloyd that afternoon. Traylor wanted to show him the copies of the letters he had sent, hoping this would pacify the miners. But neither Lloyd nor any other union representative showed up. Traylor was disappointed.

Later that afternoon Traylor was visiting a store when some miners came in demanding to know what he was going to do to restart the company. Traylor replied that he had done all he could and that he was waiting to hear from Martin. It wasn't enough. The miners demanded that Traylor start up the company or get out of town within forty-eight hours.

Traylor did not let himself be intimidated. He and his family stayed in Ely. But the miners made it clear he wasn't welcome. They left an imitation coffin on his doorstep. They broke into his office and broke all the windows. Mill machinery mysteriously broke down. One day there was an unexplained explosion. When the forty-eight hours was up in January 1903, seventy-five union men showed up at Traylor's house at three o'clock in the morning warning him to get out of town in the next twelve hours. He refused.

The miners hired two rigs from the Ely livery stable and about two dozen of them waited in a canyon that Traylor usually passed through on his way to the mine. They were set to ambush Traylor as he rode through. What they didn't know was that Sheriff Bassett had assigned a deputy to Traylor for protection. As Traylor and the deputy drove up the canyon toward the mine, the miners stopped them. They grabbed the reins of Traylor's horse but immediately let go when threatened by the deputy. Lloyd promised that he would deal with Traylor later. Traylor and the deputy rode on to the mine office.

When Traylor arrived, at least sixty men, including Lloyd, had gathered at the mill office. The deputy suggested to Traylor that they leave through a back door. Traylor was reluctant to go, afraid that the men might damage company property. The deputy decided the odds were too great against him so he abandoned Traylor to his fate. However, he did leave his gun for Traylor's use. Traylor loaded his own gun and stashed it in one coat pocket and placed the deputy's gun in the other. A few minutes later, five miners entered the mine office. They demanded to know when the mine was going to start operating again. Traylor repeated what he had told them before.

At the direction of Lloyd, who was waiting outside, two of the miners tried to grab Traylor. Traylor shot them both. Then three other men rushed in, and Traylor killed one of them and wounded the two others. The men killed were John Smith, Shamrock Johnson, and Jim Skaggs. Jim Berry later died from his wounds. Max Lambert was sent to a San Francisco hospital where he recovered.

Traylor escaped out the back door. He quickly hitched up his wagon and headed out at a gallop toward Ely. He started to follow his usual route but noticed that several armed men were waiting at the canyon, so he quickly turned the wagon around and started up the other side of the canyon. Five miles later he met two prospectors and paid them to give misinformation to the mob. He finally reached Ely after a long detour around a mountain.

The sheriff of Ely escorted Traylor to the jail by hiding him in a covered wagon. He posted guards on several roofs to shoot at any troublemakers. The miners couldn't get close to Traylor so they filled up beer kegs with dynamite to roll down to the jail. Meanwhile, a rancher named McGill furnished fast horses for the sheriff and Traylor to get out of town. The two men escaped into the night, riding 140 miles to Cherry Creek.

In a grand jury investigation Traylor submitted the letters he had written to Martin as evidence he had been trying to work with the miners. One of the miners testified that the two rigs had been hired to kidnap Traylor and take him to Wells. Finally, all charges against Traylor were dropped when the grand jury decided he was acting in self-defense. William Lloyd was indicted on a charge of attempted kidnapping. He was released on bail provided by his brother-in-law, but Lloyd did not appear for his hearing so his bail was forfeited. The entire incident was a black eye on the face of the miner's union, and it was some time before it achieved its former recognition.

Prize Fight at Goldfield
· 1906 ·

Goldfield rode a wave of prosperity during its boomtown days, but each boom has its bust. By 1906, the silver mines in the area were no longer producing much, and profits were down. Prospectors were moving on to the next town. George "Tex" Rickard, owner of the Northern Saloon, was not ready for it all to end. He had to come up with an idea to bring prosperity back to Goldfield.

He decided what Goldfield needed was a prize fight. He approached the townspeople with his idea. Many thought he was crazy, but all agreed that the town needed a boost to its economy. They also liked the idea of staying a step ahead of the nearby towns of Tonopah and Rhyolite. So Rickard was given the go-ahead.

When looking around for a fight to bring to Goldfield, he heard that Oscar "Battling" Nelson was interested in a prize fight. He called Billy Nolan, Nelson's manager, to arrange the deal. Nolan insisted on a thirty-thousand-dollar purse, and Rickard met his terms. Nelson's opponent would be Joe Gans, from Baltimore, who readily agreed to the match. Rickard picked Labor Day, September 3, 1906, as the date for the fight. He immediately began promoting the match, sending out thirty-seven thousand post-cards and thirty thousand letters across the country to generate interest in the fight that would crown the lightweight champion of the world.

In the meantime, the townspeople began building a huge arena for the fight. Anticipating that there would not be enough hotel rooms to accommodate all the visitors, the Tonopah and Goldfield Railroad built a mile of extra track on which up to three hundred Pullman cars could be parked for overnight lodging.

The fans came in droves. First the newsmen and photographers arrived. San Francisco's *Call Bulletin* erected a tent with a huge banner that said "Headquarters for the $30,000 Battle of the Century." The Biograph Company paid for the rights to film the fight to be replayed in nickelodeons across the country. The match would be one of the first championship fights ever recorded. Tickets were sold out weeks ahead of time, with some people paying twenty dollars for front row seats.

Then the fighters arrived. Gans, a thirty-two-year-old black man, had won 145 fights and lost 6. Nelson, a twenty-four-year-old white man known as "the gentle Dane" since he had emigrated from Denmark, had won 46 and lost 10. The two men worked out while waiting for the day of the fight. Gans was very accommodating and invited people into his training camp to watch him train. Nolan was not so accommodating. He roped off Nelson's training area and would not even let the press in unless they paid a one-dollar fee. The townspeople didn't like this, so then and there they started rooting for Gans, even though there was fairly strong racial prejudice at the time. That was what Nolan was hoping for because it increased the odds against Nelson.

In an inequitable split, Nelson was guaranteed to get twenty thousand dollars and Gans was to receive ten thousand dollars, no matter who won the fight. In an additional promotional gesture, engineer Malcom MacDonald, builder of the telegraph and telephone system in southern Nevada and president of the Bank of Goldfield, gave each fighter one thousand shares of mining stock that they could redeem for fifteen hundred dollars after the fight.

By the time the fight was held, over seventy thousand dollars had been collected in admissions. Boxing buffs around the country waited in eager anticipation for the bout. Those who couldn't make it to Nevada gathered around newspaper offices to get round-by-round updates. Almost seven thousand people crowded in for a ringside seat. George Siler would referee the fight.

Trying to weigh the fight in his favor, Nolan had made additional stipulations. He insisted that the men weigh in not the night before, but at ringside. He also insisted that they weigh in with trunks and shoes on. This forced Gans to fast for thirty-six hours before the fight. Gans weighed in at exactly the required 133 pounds, but he was weak from undernourishment.

The referee rang the bell and the fight was on. The fight went forty-two rounds. The two men pounded each other for almost three hours—a record for a modern championship fight. This was especially incredible for Gans, who was suffering from tuberculosis at the time. Nelson was strong but rough. Several times the referee had to stop him from butting with his head and from throwing low punches. Despite spraining his hand in the sixteenth round, Gans came close to knocking out Nelson in the twentieth round. The fight ended when Nelson hit Gans with a low foul blow. Everyone saw it, so they were not surprised or upset when the decision was given to Gans.

Nolan jumped in the ring and tried to contest the decision, claiming that the whole thing had been a fraud. He demanded that Gans forfeit his prize. Rickard refused to give in to him, so Nolan tried to sue for it. He had prints made from the fight film, blew them up to life size, and showed them around the town. He tried to prove that the referee did not have a clear view and could not have seen the supposed low blow. But a week later, a Chicago paper printed a picture that clearly showed the low blow and the argument was put to rest.

Rickard made thirteen thousand dollars on the fight. He was also successful in getting Goldfield back on the map and into the conscious of America. Goldfield was in the news again when Gans fought in Tonopah on January 1, 1907. The Goldfield newspaper spread the word of that fight in which Gans beat Kid Herman for a twelve-thousand-dollar purse. Two years later Nelson beat Gans for the lightweight championship crown, but he lost it again in 1910, when he was defeated by Al Wolgast.

Rickard would go on to promote the famous Johnson versus Jeffries fight in Reno in 1910. He would also promote the famous fight between Jack Dempsey and Gene Tunney at Madison Square Garden in New York. Goldfield never had another large fight after the Gans-Nelson match, but the local athletic clubs started staging many fights of their own.

Goldfield refused to die with the mines. Its opinion of itself was clear from the masthead of the local paper, which read, "All that's New and True of the Greatest Gold Camp Ever Known." Today Goldfield is a ghost town with only a few residents, but many of the buildings that welcomed visitors in 1906 still stand proudly.

Gold Discovered at Battle Mountain
· 1909 ·

Dora and Sherman Wilhelm and their two small children left Trenton, Missouri, in May 1896 in search of gold. Wilhelm had grown tired of his job with the Rock Island Railroad, where he protected railroad property, often chasing bandits and breaking up fights. Wilhelm thought he might like to try his hand at prospecting. His friend Frank Ransom gave him a grubstake for a forty percent share of the profits. Even though the railroad now crossed the country, the Wilhelms traveled by covered wagon, probably one of the last families to do so. Wilhelm first tried prospecting in Colorado. He worked a claim near Cripple Creek until 1900, walking away with twelve thousand dollars.

Again the family traveled by covered wagon to a camp near the Wyoming border, but they only stayed there until the spring of 1901 when they left for Idaho. The Wilhelms left Idaho in 1903 and moved to California. Wilhelm prospected awhile in the Bodie, California/Aurora, Nevada area before moving to the Carson Valley. The family stayed there until May 1907 when they headed north. They wandered all over northern Nevada—the Bull Run Mountains, the Black Rock Desert, Jack Creek, Tuscarora— looking for gold before finally arriving at Battle Mountain in August 1909.

On the big day Wilhelm and friend Dunk Duncan left town at about six o'clock in the morning to explore the Philadelphia Canyon about fourteen miles south of town. About half past nine they split up. Wilhelm wandered around several iron oxide, quartzite, and rhyolite formations. So much of it looked promising that he didn't know where to start. So he climbed a big butte to explore further and was walking along an outcropping of black rock when he decided to sit down and rest.

Suddenly he spotted a reddish clump of quartz a short distance away. He tried to kick it loose but it wouldn't budge. He pulled up the sagebrush that was growing over it but still couldn't break the rock loose. He started digging at it with his pick until he finally broke loose a couple of egg-sized pieces. When he saw them, he couldn't believe his eyes. The rocks contained pure gold! He looked around for his friend Duncan. He saw him a few hundred yards away and called him over to show him what he found.

Duncan exclaimed that he thought the ore was almost solid gold. The two men started digging, enlarging the hole until it was about a foot deep and two feet long. A gold vein three inches wide ran right through the middle of it. Duncan kept digging while Wilhelm ran back to the wagon for the two nosebags they used to feed the horses. They filled the nosebags and Wilhelm's cap with specimens.

Wilhelm had to keep the spot a secret as long as possible until the claim was properly recorded. He also needed more help and a place to live near the strike. He filled out a claim notice he always carried in his pocket and gave it to Duncan to take to town and file while he stayed at the site to keep watch.

After Duncan left, Wilhelm dug a little more in the spot. He also scouted the immediate vicinity, keeping a close lookout for claim jumpers. While he waited, Wilhelm wondered if the vein was as rich ten feet down as it was on top. He wondered if he should dig deeper right where he was or dig horizontally and take out the rich ore on top. He decided on the latter.

In the meantime, Duncan made record time back to town. He took care of the claim notice, bought supplies and food, and headed right back out to the claim. On the way, he picked up friend Ed Morath to help work the claim. Duncan and Ed returned after dark, and Wilhelm showed Morath what they had found.

The next day, the men started digging before the sun was completely up and even before they had breakfast. After breakfast, Duncan rode back to town for more supplies. Wilhelm graded an area for a shack, dug a pit for a latrine, and set up a tent for a cook shack. Morath erected the markers bordering the claim. Duncan picked up supplies and told Wilhelm's family what was happening. Then he headed back to the claim with two more men, Paul Keele and a Mr. Webster. Webster drove out a freight wagon with lumber, cots, water barrels, and other supplies. To protect his interests, Wilhelm didn't allow anyone near the strike unless he was there.

With the supplies, the men built a cabin on skids and the latrine. Wilhelm also built a table, a double bunk, and a shelf and set up a sheet-iron stove. The other men set up some tents and started building a decent road to the spot.

During all this building, the men were still prospecting. They enlarged the hole until they could see that the vein was eighteen inches wide and had a streak of high grade gold two inches thick right through the middle of it. In the first week they dug a hole eight feet long, four feet wide, and two feet deep.

Other miners started flocking to the site. After only a few days, seventeen tents and twelve frame shacks comprised the camp, now called Bannock. Special trains arrived from Austin carrying miners. Saloon keepers and merchants flocked to Bannock, hoping to cash in on the latest boom. Others brought water and sold it for twenty-five cents per canteen full, or one dollar for a bath. After two weeks, men even hauled ice packed in sawdust out to the site so that miners could have cold beer.

As he dug, Wilhelm noticed a pattern to his find. His discovery was like the hub of a wheel with spokes of rich quartz veins running in all directions. The spokes were full of gold. He also found placer gold, which yielded nuggets the size of lima beans. The placer discovery brought a whole new group of men to the area, since placer gold was much easier to work. In a few months, fifteen or twenty men were working placer claims alone. Wilhelm leased many lots on his own claim so that the gold could be harvested more quickly. He also built a furnace and smelted some of the ore right on the spot.

Bannock was one of the last big boom camps in Nevada. It is not known how much gold was taken out of the site, but assays placed it at $180,000 per ton. Several months after Wilhelm's first strike, he sold out his interest to Frank Ransom, the man who had originally given him his grubstake. The family moved on, first to California, then Arizona, where Wilhelm continued to look for another big strike.

Humboldt County Earthquake
· 1915 ·

Saturday, October 2, 1915, started just like any other day. Children were off from school, women were out shopping, and men were taking care of household repairs. But at 3:41 in the afternoon, the earth trembled beneath the feet of the residents of Humboldt County. The tremor lasted about twenty seconds. No one thought much of it, but the animals were noticeably nervous. Then came another tremor at 5:15 P.M., which lasted only three or four seconds. A few minutes later, at 5:40 P.M., a third tremor rocked the earth for three or four seconds. Then it was over. Or so it seemed until 10:54 P.M., when the big one hit!

The earthquake that struck Humboldt County that night was recorded as far away as Salt Lake City, San Diego, and Baker, Oregon. It registered 7.6 on the Richter scale. It was centered at Kennedy, a small mining town about sixty miles southwest of Winnemucca. Kennedy and ranches in the Grass Valley/Pleasant Valley area suffered the most damage.

When the earthquake hit, people woke up and rushed out into the streets in fear. The ground was moving so much that people could barely walk upright. Some people stayed awake the rest of the night, afraid of another earthquake. Some even moved their beds out into the street. The next morning the townspeople assessed the damage.

A new crack had appeared in the ground at Pleasant Valley. The crack extended twenty-five miles and ranged from six inches to twelve feet deep. The ground had sunk several inches. Another fourteen-foot-wide crack was leaking water. At Kennedy, some of the Roylance mine tunnels had caved in, and the track was covered with twelve to eighteen inches of dirt. The foundation of the mill was cracked. There was a new vertical scarp, ranging from five to twenty feet tall, that cut a twenty-two-mile-long fracture in the earth at the base of the Sonoma Range.

The Pearce Ranch was the best place to view the rift, so many people drove there to gawk at the damage. The barn had collapsed but the house was undamaged. The vibrations from the earthquake had moved heavily-loaded freight wagons across a road and into the sagebrush without leaving wheel tracks. The family remembered that the earthquake even made the moon turn color when red dust filled the air. A pet cat suffered a crushed tail but was otherwise unharmed. A creek on the property turned into a six-foot waterfall after the ground moved. Along with the new scarp, a myriad of smaller cracks crisscrossed the property. Water was seeping from many of them.

Other ranches in the area suffered considerable damage. The concrete ranch house at the nearby Cooper and Uniacke Ranch slid downhill six inches, leaving the back wall behind. The house and stables at the Siard Ranch suffered major damage. The Schell Ranch sported a new spring on the property, courtesy of a newly opened crack in the earth. The earthquake also tipped over a small house. At his ranch, Simon Reinhart discovered several large new cracks in the ground up to six hundred feet long. Water had come up through the cracks and spewed fine sand and sea shells all around.

There was other damage around Humboldt County. Many buildings in Winnemucca were severely damaged. The hardest hit was the Winneva Hall, which was used by fraternal and social organizations. Adobe buildings in Paradise Valley forty miles north of Winnemucca were damaged. At Golconda, the Southern Pacific railroad tracks sunk five inches at each end of the railroad bridge across the Humboldt River. At Battle Mountain, a sixty-five-thousand-gallon water tank crashed to the ground. Indians in the area were greatly frightened by the quake since, according to legend, an earthquake is a sign that the Great Spirit is angry. Even residents of Reno felt the earthquake. There were reports of chandeliers swinging and clocks stopping, but no real damage occurred.

Early reports placed the epicenter in various locations, some as far away as the Wasatch Mountains in Utah. However, L. St. D. Roylance, mining engineer and owner of Roylance Mines at Kennedy, knew differently. He declared that the epicenter was between Kennedy Mountain and Mount Boyer to the south. He was at Kennedy at the time and witnessed the upheaval of the mountains. The tremors there also lasted much longer than anywhere else.

Professor Jones, a prominent geologist, figured the earthquake did not occur as the result of an existing fault or slip, but from a new one. The new fault followed the base of the Sonoma Range. He concluded that the earthquake was probably as severe as the San Francisco earthquake of 1906, but the damage was much less since it occurred in a relatively remote area. He also predicted that the increase in stream flows would shortly return to normal. Even so, residents submitted fifty new applications for water rights.

There were thirty to forty aftershocks, each lasting four to five seconds, every day through the end of October. By November the aftershocks decreased to only about twelve a day, but Kennedy residents continued to feel aftershocks daily until June 1916. The Roylance Mines stopped operations "until the earth ceased moving." Winnemucca was also rocked by aftershocks for several months though none of them caused any damage.

Stage Robbed at Jarbidge
· 1916 ·

The night of December 5, 1916, was a cold one. It had been snowing since mid-afternoon on top of a snow pack that was already three feet deep. An icy wind was blowing and the temperature was dropping with the darkness. Road conditions were hazardous, so it was not too surprising that the evening stage from Rogerson, Idaho, was a little late.

But then it got to be very late, and Postmaster Scott Fleming got worried. He asked Frank Leonard to ride up the Crippen Grade, which steeply descended into town, and see if he could discover what was holding up the stage. A few hours later Leonard came back. He had ridden all the way to the top of the grade but did not see the stage.

Fleming called Mrs. Dexter, who lived on the north edge of town, and asked her if she had seen the stage come in. She reported that the stage had passed her place about suppertime. This was very curious. Her house was only one-half mile from the post office. Yet the stage had still not arrived. Fleming began to suspect foul play.

He organized a search party of about a dozen men. They searched the canyon between Mrs. Dexter's house and the post office. In a few minutes they found the stagecoach abandoned near some willow trees. The driver, Fred Searcy, lay dead on the front seat. He had been shot in the head. The horses were still tied to a nearby tree. The robber had cut open the second-class mail sack and thrown the contents on the ground. It was later discovered that he had also cut open the first-class mail sack and stolen $2,800 in cash that belonged to Crumley & Walker's Success Bar and Café.

The storm was getting worse so no more searching was done that night. Guards were posted all over town to make sure no one left. The next morning the search party discovered where the killer had waited for the stagecoach beside the road. Evidently he jumped on the stage as it went past. He must have shot the driver while the stage was still moving then took the reins himself. Two sets of footprints, a set of dog tracks, and a trail of blood led through the trees and across a bridge.

Under the bridge the search party found a blood-soaked overcoat, a sack of coins worth about three hundred dollars, a bag of registered mail, and the stage driver's cap. They also found a white shirt and blue bandana weighted down with stones in the stream.

While the men were searching, a stray dog that was known in town ran off into the brush and started digging in the snow. The dog uncovered the first-class mail sack which was covered with blood stains. It seemed a great coincidence that the dog knew the location of the mail sack, so the search party suspected the dog might provide an important clue to the identity of the criminal.

Someone remembered that the dog often followed Ben Kuhl, a local miner who wasn't very well liked, possibly because of a claim-jumping incident. He had been free on bail while appealing a four-hundred-dollar fine. The man's need for money, the dog's friendship with him, and the fact that he wore shirts similar to the one found was enough to bring him under suspicion. A few days later he was arrested for robbery of the U.S. mail and for murder.

Kuhl formerly worked as a cook at the O.K. Mine. He had recently quit that job and moved to town with Ed Beck and Billy McGraw. When police searched their cabin, they found a .44-

caliber revolver. The hammer rested on one spent cartridge. The gun belonged to Beck, who had loaned it to McGraw a month earlier. McGraw usually left the gun with the bartender at the Success Bar in the morning and picked it up from him each night. The night of the Searcy killing, Beck had asked McGraw for the gun saying Kuhl wanted it for hunting. McGraw got the gun from the bartender and gave it to Beck. About eight o'clock that night, just before the body was found, Beck and Kuhl entered the Jack Griffin saloon and bought a round of drinks. They wanted to attract a lot of attention to the fact that they were there and what time it was.

Several friends provided an alibi for Kuhl, but the towns-people wanted to believe he had committed the crime. Kuhl, Beck, and McGraw were all arrested. McGraw was later released.

Kuhl was tried at Elko, the county seat. Forty-six witnesses testified at the three-week trial. C. H. Stone, supervisor of the Bureau of Identification in Bakersfield, California, testified for the prosecution. He was a fingerprint expert who had been asked to study the bloody palm print found on a piece of the first-class mail. He identified eighteen points on the palm print used for identification and matched them to Kuhl's hand. Kuhl's attorneys argued that the palm print was not admissible evidence, but the judge ruled it would be allowed. This ruling set a precedent for such prints to be used in later trials. On October 7, 1917, Kuhl was found guilty of both the murder and the robbery of the U.S. mail. He was sentenced to death. The date of his execution was set for January 1918.

Then Beck's trial began. His attorneys argued that he couldn't have been there when the stage was robbed and the driver shot. They said another man who was still at large was involved. They also argued that the hole in Searcy's cap was too small to have been caused by a bullet from a .44-caliber gun. The only thing they admitted was that Beck knew about Kuhl's plan but chose to keep quiet because Kuhl threatened to kill him. Beck was found guilty, too; he received a life sentence.

On December 17, 1917, Kuhl's attorney applied for a stay of execution, stating that there were sixty-one errors during the trial, the foremost being the admission of a person's palm print as evidence. The stay was granted so that an appeal could be filed. The appeal was heard on September 6, 1918, but the supreme court upheld the decision of the district court. Kuhl's execution date was again set.

On December 10, 1918, Kuhl and his attorneys met with the state to confess what happened. He said that he and Searcy had set up the whole thing to look like someone else did it. But when they went to pull the job they got into an argument, and Searcy would not turn over the $2,800 in registered mail. While fighting for the money, they went for their guns and Kuhl shot Searcy. Because of this confession, Kuhl's sentence was converted to life in prison. He spent twenty-seven years in the state prison at Carson City before being released in 1944. He died six months later in Sacramento.

The stolen $2,800 was never found. It was never proven that there was a fourth party involved as Ed Beck claimed. The event will always be remembered as the last stage robbery in the United States in which the driver was killed. It was also the first case in which a palm print was used to convict a criminal.

The Winning of Barbara Worth
· 1926 ·

In 1926, movie scouts came to Nevada looking for the perfect place to film Hollywood's next great epic. Producer Samuel Goldwyn and his director, Henry King, wanted a realistic desert location for their film, *The Winning of Barbara Worth*, an adaptation of the book written by Harold Bell Wright. The book told a tale of claiming the desert for agricultural purposes. The story's characters diverted the Colorado River into canals and pipes to accomplish this great task. Nevada had plenty of desert sites to choose from.

King and two associates arrived in Reno on April 14, 1926. They scouted several areas but thought the Black Rock Desert and the small town of Gerlach would be perfect. Producer Goldwyn joined King, and they rented a car and scouted the desert scenery around Wadsworth and Lovelock. On the way to Gerlach, the car's radiator boiled over. They found some water in a nearby hot spring. But they had to wait several hours before the water was cool enough to use. They finally arrived in Gerlach at half past ten that night. Despite their troubles getting there, Goldwyn liked the location. The town could accommodate the film crew, and the desert around it was exactly what he wanted. He went back to Oakland to plan the shoot.

The Winnemucca Chamber of Commerce and Mayor Carlton E. Haviland helped Goldwyn find office space and filming locations. Lovelock rancher W. H. Cooper supplied livestock, such as horses, pack mules, and burros. P. A. Quigley supplied one hundred tons of hay for the livestock. The motion picture company United Artists rented twenty-five wagons, buggies, and freight wagons from the locals. In the meantime, King set up an office at Hotel Humboldt and hired about fifty men, women, and children as extras.

The set designers arrived in Gerlach on June 13. They built a false-front city. The lumber was hauled in by railroad since there were no trees in the area. A second false-front city was built at Trego. Besides the buildings, crews built new water mains to create the flood scenes that were part of the story. A third false-front city was built near Blue Mountain, west of Winnemucca. These three false-front cities would become the fictitious towns of Rubio City, Kingston, San Felipe, and other smaller towns created by Wright.

The film production process was extremely well organized. King declared alcohol off limits at the filming locations. He hired two agents from the Nevada Prohibition Administrator to ensure the camps stayed "dry," and he imposed a curfew. Cast and crew were required to take all meals at the mess tent. Men and women were not allowed in each other's quarters. King carefully rationed water, since it cost $150 per tanker load to be hauled out to the site. United Artists established infirmaries for treating any illnesses or injuries.

The actors and the rest of the crew arrived in Nevada on June 21. Ronald Colman and Vilma Banky played the leads in the story. Colman was Willard Holmes, an engineer working for a big eastern firm that would build the system of canals to irrigate the desert. Banky played Barbara Worth, to whom all the male characters dedicated their work. Gary Cooper played a man named Abe Lee in the film—one of his first roles.

King wanted to start filming on June 20, but set changes and costume alterations cost him an extra day. But when filming began, a large crowd was on hand to watch the first take. Right away there was a problem. A wagon overturned when the horses pulling it were spooked. Six people fell out and the driver was knocked unconscious. Fortunately, no one was badly hurt.

The next day, a sandstorm blew up. King was thrilled that nature was cooperating. A huge sandstorm figured into the first part of the story in which Barbara Worth, as a young child, is lost in the desert. He ordered a crew to drive around the desert and film the storm. The wind blew down several buildings and tents. A rainstorm immediately followed the dust storm, washing out the road to Gerlach. Production was set back three days. On June 24, when shooting resumed, a man lost control of his horses and his wagon raced out of control through the middle of town. King also recorded that incident on film. He remained unperturbed by the disasters; they could be used in the final cut.

The actors took a break on July 4, but they were right back at it the next day. When the temperature reached 124 degrees, King changed the shooting schedule to begin at five o'clock in the morning. He moved the curfew from ten o'clock to nine. Another mishap occurred on July 6 when cook Walter Ordson accidentally set the commissary tent on fire. The commissary tent, a sleeping tent, and two storage shelters burned down before the fire was put out. This didn't ruffle King at all. By July 8, he had the crew back out filming another sandstorm. In the meantime, he needed more extras. He could not find all the men he needed at Winnemucca, so he sent a man to Reno to hire some more. A special train transported them to Winnemucca.

When Governor James G. Scrugham visited the set on July 18, King gave him a tour and kept him on hand to watch the filming. That same day crews were loading a train to take all their gear to Winnemucca. The next scene to be filmed was the bandit ambush. The sequence was shot at Devil's Canyon, sixty miles south of Winnemucca. Coincidentally, this is the name of the place the ambush took place in Wright's book. There were no major mishaps during this part of the filming, though the crew did have to ride to the locale on horseback and pack in the equipment on mules. While crews shot the ambush, other crews took pictures of Paradise Valley, where there were acres of cultivated fields and orchards. The last scenes in the desert were finished on August 4. Banky was injured that day when a horse stepped on her.

King picked the St. Paul's Catholic Church in Winnemucca as the place for the wedding scene between Colman and Valmy. The church's real priest, Father Hugo A. Meisekothen, performed the ceremony. King used a bit of creative license here, as Wright's book does not actually end in their wedding, and after the editing process, the wedding scene did not appear in the film. Most of the cast left Nevada that evening.

The film debuted in Los Angeles on October 14. Previews lauded the film as a great western. Reviewers loved the actors' performances. King was applauded for filming in Nevada rather than on a set and for his special effects.

On December 7, the film opened at the American Theater in Winnemucca. Before the first showing, the theater manager read a telegram sent by Colman and Banky thanking the citizens for their cooperation. The editor of the *Humboldt Star* figured the movie would help congress see the possibilities of irrigating the desert. His prediction came true only a few years later when the government built the mighty Hoover Dam to tap the Colorado River.

Giant Diversion Tunnels Dug for Hoover Dam

· 1932 ·

The building of Hoover Dam was an ambitious project. This huge concrete structure would bring electricity and irrigation to the southwestern desert. It would control the seasonal flooding of the Colorado River, and it would put thousands of Depression-era people to work. Black Canyon was chosen as the dam site because it would impound the largest amount of water. It also had stable geology, with rock walls consisting of volcanic andesite. But before the dam could be built, the water had to be diverted from Black Canyon. Four massive diversion tunnels, two on each side of the river, would have to be built through the solid rock walls.

A consortium, Six Companies Inc., bid on the project and won the largest federal contract granted up to that time. The six companies in this consortium were W. A. Bechtel of San Francisco and Henry J. Kaiser of Oakland; Utah Construction Company of Ogden, Utah; MacDonald & Kahn Company of Los Angeles; Morrison-Knudsen Company of Boise; J. F. Shea Company of Portland, Oregon; and Pacific Bridge Company of Portland, Oregon. All of them had years of experience in building everything from highways to tunnels to dams. Frank T. Crowe was the lead engineer.

Before work could begin on the tunnels, highways and railroads had to be built to the dam site so materials and men could be transported there. But the men working on the tunnels did not wait for the roads and rails. About two miles upriver, trucks brought portable air compressors and drilling tools to the shore where they were loaded onto barges and floated to the dam site.

The mouths of the tunnels started two thousand feet upstream from the dam site. They would be fifty feet in diameter with a combined length of 15,909 feet.

First, workers drilled adits into the canyon walls perpendicular to the middle of the tunnels. This way, men could work from the middle of the tunnel to each end while, at the same time, other men worked at each end moving toward the middle. They drilled the first adit on the Arizona side of the river on May 12, 1931. After finishing that side, the men built a cable suspension footbridge across the river to blast the adits on the Nevada side. They accomplished this work with no electricity; the tools were powered by two two-hundred-horsepower diesel engines. Electricity in the form of power lines extended from California arrived on June 25, 1931, at which time the tools were converted to run on that power source.

Three shifts worked around the clock to excavate the tunnels. Crowe invented a contraption called a drill carriage, or jumbo, that allowed them to excavate more quickly. This contraption consisted of a framework made of wood—later of welded steel—on top of a World War I truck chassis. Each jumbo had five bars with six 144-pound pneumatic drills mounted on each bar. A compressor station on each side of the river supplied power for the drills. The jumbo was then backed into the tunnel with men aboard. Twenty-two miners, twenty-one chuck tenders, five nippers, one safety miner, and one drilling foreman could work from the jumbo at one time. They used forty percent gelatin dynamite to blast the tough spots.

While crews kept drilling the tunnels, other crews hauled the debris away. Each "mucking" crew at each end of the tunnel had eight one-hundred-ton mechanical shovels at its disposal. Dump trucks hauled the rocks and dirt two miles up the river to help build the railroad bed there. Other debris was piled into the river to help build a formation for the cofferdams, which would help divert water to the tunnels. Later, ten-ton locomotives and dump cars hauled debris away to the top of the canyon.

It was a tough, dirty, and dangerous job, and the pressure of the deadlines rushed jobs and sacrificed safety. State law prohibited gas trucks in the tunnels but Six Companies claimed it was a federal project so they were exempt from the law. Men were frequently rushed to the hospital with carbon monoxide poisoning, and some died from it. There were rumors that Six Companies covered up such deaths and blamed them on pneumonia. Men had to constantly watch out for loose and sharp rocks that would fall from the cave walls. The summer of 1931 was one of the hottest on record, with an average high temperature of 119 degrees Fahrenheit and an average daily low temperature of 95 degrees Fahrenheit. Men collapsed on the job. Some had to be packed in ice to cool them down so they would survive. Fourteen men died from heat exhaustion and dehydration.

On August 7, 1931, Six Companies reassigned some men to lower paying jobs. This caused the Industrial Workers of the World union to send the entire work force out on strike. They demanded cold drinking water at the job site, a flat rate for board, an eight-hour day, higher wages, and several safety improvements, including removing electrical lines from wet areas and moving dynamite away from the work site. After six days, the strike collapsed. Six Companies suspended men suspected of being union members. At the beginning of 1932, Six Companies did move the men and their families from the dam site to the government town at Boulder City, which greatly improved living conditions.

In February 1932, further excavation was delayed when the Colorado River flooded, sending fifty thousand cubic feet of water per second through the tunnels. There wasn't much damage, but both water and sediment had to be pumped out of the tunnels so work could continue. By that time the major excavation was complete, but the surface had to be smoothed and evened out. Six Companies used a specially-designed trimming jumbo for the job. Then the tunnels were ready to be lined with concrete.

Six Companies designed its own molds since there was nothing available on such a scale. The concrete was mixed a short distance upstream from the tunnel mouth on the Nevada side. Trucks drove over a suspension bridge to pour concrete on the Arizona side. Two concrete strips served as rails for the gantry cranes, which transported the concrete within the tunnels. Originally fifty-six feet in diameter, the tunnels were reduced to fifty feet by the three feet of concrete that lined them. On November 13, 1932, the tunnel on the Arizona side was filled with water for the first time.

For the next two years water from the Colorado River was diverted so the dam could be constructed. On February 1, 1935, just before the dam was finished, the inner diversion tunnels were filled with concrete and blocked with steel gates. When the dam was completed in May 1935, the two outer diversion tunnels became the dam's spillways.

The dam was finished two years ahead of schedule. The desert bloomed. The cities lit up. The floods were over. Today Arizona, Colorado, New Mexico, Utah, California, Nevada, Wyoming, and Mexico all benefit from the resources of the mighty Colorado River.

The Kidnapping of Roy Frisch

· 1934 ·

In 1909, the Nevada legislature passed an anti-gambling law. The law pleased those who had been on an anti-gambling crusade, but it had an immediate unfavorable impact on the economy of some cities, including Reno. Several years later, the legislature began to allow some gambling, but prizes could not exceed two dollars. Slot machines could not pay off in cash. Poker and blackjack were allowed only if a different dealer dealt every hand. But the hardcore gambler sought higher stakes. Such stakes were generally available in Reno, in hidden corners and back rooms. Bill Graham and Jim McKay owned the largest of these hidden clubs, known as the Bank Club. Graham and McKay had several notorious friends, such as Baby Face Nelson and Pretty Boy Floyd, who used to hang out at their club while they were hiding from the law.

In the early 1930s, Graham and McKay hatched a scheme. They promised investors high returns if they would deposit their money and securities in the Riverside Bank in Reno. In exchange for these securities, the investors received a worthless piece of paper. Graham and McKay immediately sent the securities to New York for sale. It wasn't long before Graham, McKay, and their four New York partners were arrested for using the mail to defraud. Graham and McKay were also involved in a scheme that cheated bettors out of winnings from horse races and cheated investors out of gains from insider stock trading. The Riverside Bank laundered their cash, checks, and securities.

Graham and McKay's New York partners were indicted in 1933 and convicted largely on the testimony of Roy Frisch, a Riverside Bank cashier. Then it came time to try Graham and McKay. The trial of the two men was set for June 1934. Arraignment was scheduled for April 2.

At the time, Frisch lived with his mother Barbara and sisters Alice and Louisa at 247 Court Street. On March 22, the women decided to have a bridge party. Choosing not to join them, Frisch elected to see a movie instead. He decided to walk to the movie theater, which was just a few blocks away. He left home about a quarter to eight that night but he did not return after the movie. His mother waited up for him for a little while but finally gave up and went to bed, leaving the porch light on.

The next day, she reported Frisch missing. Local and county police started an immediate investigation. First they retraced the route that Frisch likely walked to and from the theater. They speculated that he had walked downtown two blocks east on Court to Virginia Street and turned north at the courthouse. From there, he would have walked past the Riverside Bank and crossed the Truckee River bridge. He probably would have turned east on First and walked two blocks to the Majestic Theater. The theater manager thought he remembered seeing Frisch in the theater. Several friends said they saw him walking home just after ten o'clock. Harry B. Gorline was probably the last person to see Frisch alive, at the corner of Sierra and Court. But somewhere between Sierra Street and his home, Frisch disappeared.

Newspapers that reported on Frisch's disappearance described his physical appearance and what he was wearing. County commissioners offered a reward of one thousand dollars for any information about the case.

Fisch had disappeared just a few days before his scheduled testimony in federal court against McKay and Graham. Investigators speculated that Graham and McKay and their gangster friends had kidnapped Frisch.

A citywide search began. Everyone from the American Legion to the local Boy Scouts joined in. Police searched abandoned speakeasies, and the county sheriff dragged the Truckee River. They searched old mines, including a mine off Hunter Creek Road southwest of town. Tire tracks led to one of its shafts. There Deputy Cliff Duclose found a bloody hat and three pistol shell casings. Empty pistol cartridges and bloody rags also turned up at the Black Panther Mine. Police searched some abandoned shacks at Fort Churchill where lights and cars had been reported on the night Frisch disappeared, but they found nothing there.

The only real tip came from Mrs. M. E. Nicol, who lived at 225 Court Street. She said about half past eight that night a man came to her door looking for a certain address on Court Street. She said a dark car was parked at the curb. But the information led to nothing. Reno police found a suspicious note that had both Frisch's name and District Attorney Melvin Jepson's name on it, but Frisch's name had been crossed off. After that Jepson installed heavy shades on his office windows. Police stationed a guard outside the home of Frisch's assistant cashier, Joseph Fuetsch, who was also scheduled to testify.

The police investigated Baby Face Nelson and an accomplice named John Paul Chase. Nelson and Chase had been in town that day and left the city on March 23. Chase met with Graham at the Sir Francis Drake Hotel in San Francisco the following day.

In the meantime, the trial of Graham and McKay commenced on June 4. Defense lawyers tried to show that Frisch was a key figure in the swindle, but Joseph Fuetsch testified that he believed Frisch had been killed to keep him quiet. The trial ended in a hung jury. Graham and McKay were finally convicted in a third trial in 1937. After their appeals, Graham and McKay were sentenced to nine years in Leavenworth and fined eleven thousand dollars each. They were released in 1945. They took over operation of the Cal-Neva Lodge at Lake Tahoe and the Bank Club in Reno. McKay died on June 20, 1962, and Graham died on November 5, 1965.

If Baby Face Nelson ever had anything to do with Frisch's disappearance, he received his just punishment long before he would have been tried. On November 27, 1934, he was killed in a shootout with two federal agents in Barrington, Illinois. On July 13, 1935, Chase admitted to being with Nelson when Nelson kidnapped Frisch, but he told two different versions of the story. In the first, Nelson forced Frisch into the car, drove to a garage, and killed him. In another version, Frisch tried to escape from the moving car, fell out near Sparks, and injured himself, then died a few minutes later from his injuries. In either case, the two men buried the body. Chase was later asked to help find the location of the body, but he could not remember exactly where it was. A rumor suggested that Frisch's body could be found at the Adelaide Mine near Winnemucca.

In 1941, Frisch was declared legally dead. Sister Louisa kept the porch light on for years hoping that her brother would return. The family always felt that Graham, McKay, and Nelson were responsible and that Frisch had no involvement whatsoever in the mail fraud scheme.

Henderson Supports War Effort
· 1943 ·

During World War II, the United States became concerned when German aircraft appeared to be superior to American-made aircraft. When a German plane was shot down, America discovered the secret of the German aircraft. The plane was made of a magnesium alloy which made it much lighter, faster, and more maneuverable than any American plane. Suddenly America had found a new use for magnesium. But at the time, only one or two United States companies specialized in producing magnesium products.

Industrialist Howard P. Eells, president of Basic Refractories Inc. in Cleveland, Ohio, knew a lot about magnesium. He approached the federal government about building a huge magnesium processing plant. Eells already knew where he could find the mineral. Two years before, he had sent geologists to Nye County, Nevada, to search for heat-resistant materials for his manufacturing company. While exploring Gabbs Valley, Nevada, the geologists had discovered a huge deposit of brucite and magnesite, which could be used to make a magnesium alloy. Eells signed an agreement between Basic Refractories Inc. and the federal government in April 1941. He formed Basic Magnesium Inc. (BMI) to manage the job.

The Defense Plant Corporation supervised the building of two plants. Located about 330 miles away from Las Vegas, the Gabbs plant was so remote that its water came from wells and electricity was purchased from Tonopah, sixty-four miles away. Construction began in the fall of 1941, with major processes ready about a year later. Macdonald Engineering Company of Chicago built the plant along with supporting office buildings, housing, and mess hall facilities. The plant would take ore through its first stage by converting it to magnesium oxide by separating and heating.

Next the ore would be shipped to a large plant which was going to be built halfway between Hoover Dam and Las Vegas to take advantage of the cheap electrical power and the abundant water supply. Part of the project would include building water and transmission lines from Hoover Dam to the plant. This plant would process the magnesium oxide into "cheeses" that could be molded into war materials. The powdered magnesium oxide was mixed with crushed coal and peat moss to provide porosity. This mixture was formed into briquettes that were heated and fed into chlorinators, where they were mixed with chlorine to form magnesium chloride pellets. Then an electrical current was passed through the pellets to separate the pellets into metallic magnesium and chlorine gas. The gas was recycled to the chlorinators while the metallic magnesium was molded into five-pound ingots.

The McNeil Construction Company of Los Angeles built the main plant on 2,800 acres of undeveloped land that would become the town of Henderson. Construction started in September 1941. Workers from all over the country were hired to build the plant. Unlike other government wartime projects, in which workers did not know what they were working on, workers at BMI knew exactly what they were producing. A training department provided orientation to new employees and explained what magnesium was, how it was used, and how it would be processed.

McNeil built several buildings to process the magnesium ore: a preparation plant, an electrolysis building, two huge chlorination plants, refineries, and a flux plant. The Defense Plant Corporation built over five hundred houses for the employees. By the end of March 1942, the Defense Plant Corporation had also completed a fourteen-mile-long, forty-inch-wide pipeline from Lake Mead to the site. This line could transport thirty million gallons of water per day. The power lines were completed about the same time.

The magnesium plant was finished in May 1943. The finished structure was one and three-quarters of a mile long and three-quarters of a mile wide, ten times the size originally designed. An amazing twenty million bricks were used in the construction of the plant and several support buildings. Seven hundred different shapes and sizes of bricks were used, some weighing as much as 110 pounds, and some with as many as fifteen sides. The bricks were shipped in from all over the country and some cost as much as twelve dollars each.

Even before the plant was finished, BMI started processing ore. In October 1942, about the time Eells sold the company to the Anaconda Copper Mining Company, the first ingots were made from the ore shipped from Gabbs. Concern about wartime gas and rubber rationing led the company to ship the ore by rail rather than drive trucks the 330 miles to Henderson. But there was no direct route, so the ore was driven to the railroad depot at Luning, about twenty-five miles away, then shipped by train 1,100 miles through northern Nevada to Ogden, Utah, and then south to Henderson. Later the company started using the highway to transport ore directly to Henderson.

Men worked for 807 consecutive days processing magnesium. During those 807 days, the plant produced 166,322,685 pounds of magnesium ingots. The ingots were shipped around the country to make into war materials such as incendiary bombs and aerial flares. The plant produced so much magnesium so quickly that the federal government decided it did not need any more and stopped production on November 15, 1944.

After the war, most of the plant's employees moved away from the area and half of the homes stood empty. The federal government wanted to dismantle the plant and sell it for scrap, but the state government decided to buy the plant for twenty-four million dollars. The state then sold it to Basic Management Incorporated, which took over management of the plant, several thousand acres of land, and the utilities. Much of the original plant is still being used today in a variety of industrial applications.

The plant at Gabbs ceased production after the war, and most families left when they realized there would be no post-war mission. Some of the housing units were shipped to the nearby Fallon military training facility, which badly needed lodgings. The city of Tonopah also bought a few housing units. Other interests soon started carting away entire buildings until a few individuals tried to save the town before it was completely hauled away. In 1947, the plant was transferred to the Guy F. Atkinson Company. It was saved and still produces magnesite ore for civilian use today.

Bugsy Builds the Flamingo
· 1946 ·

When mobster Benjamin "Bugsy" Siegel arrived in Las Vegas in 1945, it was still a small town. It had grown up from a railroad town in the early twentieth century and clung to its Old West roots. Siegel saw the city as the ticket to the end of his problems. Indicted on a California murder and released due to lack of evidence, he figured it was time to get out of the state. The mob had long had its hand in gambling, and a Las Vegas casino seemed the perfect way to continue their success.

But rather than sticking to the Old West theme of the rest of Las Vegas casinos, Siegel wanted to create a much more upscale establishment. He wasn't interested in attracting the locals. He wanted his new casino and hotel to attract wealthy Los Angeles and Florida travelers. This casino and luxury hotel would have all the amenities. It would be the type of place where men wore tuxedos and women dressed in evening gowns. It would be the first hotel to have a showroom, and Siegel intended to hire top-name entertainment.

Seven miles outside of town was a setup tailor-made for Siegel's plans. Billy Wilkerson, a Los Angeles businessman and restaurateur was building a hotel and casino named the Flamingo. Wilkerson was a compulsive gambler, sometimes gambling up to fifty thousand dollars in one day. He had started building the casino so that he could own the house where he gambled. But by January 1945, he found himself short of the money needed to finish the project. Siegel stepped in.

With the backing of mob bosses Charles "Lucky" Luciano and Meyer Lansky, Siegel invested in the casino. He hired a publicist named Francis Kilduff. At that time, Las Vegas was still largely a Mormon town, so Kilduff adopted the name of Brigham Townsend, a Mormon prophet, thinking he would be more successful. It seemed to work. Many businesses seemed willing to do business with Siegel. For example, a local dairy got the contract to supply milk and Siegel's favorite yogurt to the Flamingo. Local law enforcement agreed to leave Siegel alone as long as he kept his crime out of town. Siegel took up residence at the construction site.

Siegel really knew nothing about construction, business, or casinos. He promised his investors that the Flamingo would open on December 26, 1946. It was a promise he shouldn't have made, because after World War II, building supplies were very hard to obtain. Nevada Senator Pat McCarran used his influence to relax restrictions on construction materials, so Siegel was able to buy building supplies, but Siegel had to pay outrageous prices. Sometimes he was tricked into paying two or three times for the same thing. One time, some palm trees were delivered, taken away at night and hidden, and then returned the next day. Since Siegel didn't check his inventory or bills of lading, he paid for them again. He insisted on the most expensive furnishings, which inflated his bill even more. There were several construction errors. Even his personal suite was not immune; the beam for the ceiling was set at five feet, eight inches, too short for his height of five feet, ten inches.

Within a few months the project was three million dollars over budget, and the Flamingo was still not finished. Lansky would not give Siegel any more money. Siegel pressured Wilkerson into giving up the rest of his shares in the company to placate his mob bosses. Wilkerson did, under threat of death. But Siegel was still worried that the mob was going to come after him. He built secret passages into the hotel, adding even more cost. He designed his suite with three-foot-thick concrete walls, side exits, and trap doors in the closets. He instructed engineer Don Garwin to change the locks on his room almost every week.

The Flamingo opened as scheduled on December 26, 1946, but only the casino, restaurant, and showroom were ready. Siegel's mob partners wanted him to wait until the hotel rooms were ready too, but he refused to listen. The Flamingo sported a giant pink neon sign and replicas of pink flamingos on the lawn and a gorgeous outdoor pool surrounded with palm trees. Siegel also planted a rose garden in honor of his girlfriend Virginia Hill.

But it was a bad day for an opening; there was a huge rainstorm. Bandleader Xavier Cugat and comedian Jimmy Durante performed, but most of the other celebrities Siegel had invited couldn't make it because flights wouldn't leave Los Angeles in the storm. Most of the customers were curious locals, not the high-class clientele that Siegel had planned. A black cat had kittens in the hotel fountain. Rather than move the cats, considered bad luck, the fountain was not turned on.

Over the next few days it was obvious that lack of hotel rooms was a problem. Those who might have come to play at the Flamingo also needed to stay overnight there, but there were few hotel rooms nearby. At that time, the Flamingo was one of the only businesses on "the Strip," several miles from anything else. Finally, in February, Siegel closed the Flamingo for a month to finish construction. The Flamingo reopened with seventy-seven hotel rooms for rent in March 1947. The Andrews Sisters were the headlining entertainment.

Finally the hotel and casino started to make money, but it wasn't fast enough to suit the mob. The mob bosses heard rumors that Siegel and/or his girlfriend Virginia Hill were skimming from the profits. The mob knew they wouldn't be able to convince Siegel to step out of operations and just collect profits. They had to get rid of him.

On June 20, Siegel returned to Los Angeles to take care of some business. Afterward, he retired to his girlfriend's Beverly Hills mansion with some friends. At about half past ten o'clock at night, as he sat reading the *Los Angeles Times*, Siegel was shot and killed. He was buried in a five-thousand-dollar silver-plated casket. There were only five mourners at his funeral. California hitman Frankie Carbo was the suspected killer, but he was never charged.

Gus Greenbaum stepped in and took over the Flamingo until 1958, when he and his wife were murdered. The hotel changed hands several times before 1967, when billionaire Kirk Kerkorian bought it. Hit by hard times, Kerkorian had to sell it in 1971 at a very low price to the Hilton Hotels Corporation.

The Flamingo now grosses millions of dollars each year. Just recently, the Flamingo was renovated for $130 million. The last bit of Siegel's legacy, the "Bugsy Bungalow," also known as the Oregon Building, was finally demolished. A memorial to Siegel— a stone pillar and a small plaque—was erected in the rose garden. About the same time, the Bugsy Celebrity Theater was opened, prompted by the 1991 movie *Bugsy*. With expansions in 1977, 1980, 1982, 1986, 1990, and 1993, the Flamingo now boasts six high-rise towers with 3,642 rooms, making it the fourth largest hotel in the world.

Operation Ranger
· 1951 ·

In December 1950, the U.S.S.R. exploded its first atomic bomb, increasing pressure on the United States to develop a supply of nuclear weapons. The United States had tested bombs in the South Pacific, but that was so far away that the tests were very expensive and security was difficult to maintain. In 1947, Project Nutmeg was formed to search for a place to test atomic bombs in the United States.

On December 21, 1950, the Atomic Energy Commission and the United States Air Force set aside 350 square miles of Nevada desert to test atomic bombs. They chose this site because it was the largest of the areas being studied, it was already under federal control, and Nellis Air Force Base was close by. Construction of a test site in Nevada also had the support of Nevada Senator Pat McCarran, who felt the federal jobs would be good for the economy. The dry weather was favorable and prevailing winds would carry any fallout into uninhabited areas.

On January 11, 1951, the Atomic Energy Commission distributed a handbill that warned citizens to keep away from the area where the tests would be conducted. This was the first time the public knew about the tests, but they were generally supportive because they felt the work was necessary for national security.

Operation Ranger was the code name given to the first five tests, which would begin January 27, 1951. The official purpose of the tests was "to provide sufficient data to determine satisfactory design criteria for nuclear devices." The code names for the five tests were Able, Baker, Easy, Baker-2, and Fox.

Before the tests were conducted, the government built fourteen shelters between zero and 1.13 miles from ground zero. They also built one one-man foxhole, ten two-man foxholes, and three prone shelters. The foxholes were only about six feet long by two feet wide by four feet deep. The holes were lined with plywood to keep them from collapsing. One hundred different fabrics were laid out on panels at various distances from the blast site. This was an experiment by the army to develop fireproof clothing for its soldiers. Forty-one film badges were laid at ninety-eight-yard intervals away from ground zero to measure radioactivity. Test crews measured background radiation for a two-hundred-mile radius around ground zero.

The day before the test, the one-thousand-pound bomb was transported from Sandia Corporation in New Mexico to Kirtland Air Force Base. The bomb was outfitted with a barometer, timer, and radar units. The barometer would ensure that the bomb didn't explode until it reached a specific atmospheric pressure. The radar units in the tail were a backup in case the barometric unit failed. The bomb was loaded into a B-50 bomber. Forty-five minutes before takeoff, officials from the Los Alamos Laboratory delivered the nuclear capsule. The two pieces were kept separate until just before the drop.

The bomber and an escort bomber took off at 1:15 A.M. They arrived at Indian Springs Air Force Base near the test site at 3:45 A.M. At 3:50 A.M. the men began assembling the bomb, and at 4:34 A.M., they were finished. The pilot ascended to 19,700 feet. He flew two practice runs over the drop zone. The other B-50 followed the first to take pictures of the drop, which occurred at 5:45 A.M. The bomb exploded 1,060 feet above the ground.

Able was the first atomic explosion in the United States since the Alamogordo test in 1946. People in Las Vegas and Henderson saw the bright light and felt the concussion. The fireball rose seventeen thousand feet in the air. Immediately after the explosion, two B-29 bombers flew into the cloud to collect air samples with two collectors mounted on the top of the fuselage and one below the tail. At 6:45 A.M., two planes flew over roads adjacent to the site to measure radioactivity there.

People as far away as Salt Lake City, San Diego, San Francisco, Fresno, Needles, and Los Angeles saw and heard the atomic explosion. Windows rattled in St. George, Utah. One humorous report told of a gambler who was going to sue the government because the shock waves from the explosion bounced a pair of dice from a seven to "snake-eyes" and he lost everything.

An hour after the explosion the cloud was still visible. A B-29 flew alongside the cloud, but not in it, to track its movement. That plane followed the cloud to the Sangre de Cristo Mountains south of Denver, where it had to land for fuel.

By January 29, the cloud reached the East Coast. Officials at the Eastman Kodak Headquarters in Rochester, New York, contacted the Atomic Energy Commission, alarmed at the sudden rise in radiation. George Eastman had specifically built his plant in Rochester because of the extremely low level of background radiation. Radiation damaged film so the company constantly monitored it. Scientists measured the snow that occurred just after the high levels of radiation was detected. It was very "hot," meaning it contained high levels of radiation.

By the time the radiation was being picked up on the East Coast, a second bomb, code-named Baker, had been dropped. Easy, Baker-2, and Fox were dropped shortly afterwards. Special Air Force squadrons called "Larks" tracked the clouds. Certain weather stations around the country were given special steel pots with funnels and filters to collect air and water samples. The fifth and final test bomb, Fox, was detonated on February 6. Despite warnings to stay away, the highway was lined with hundreds of cars loaded with people watching the explosion.

Amazingly, the Las Vegas Chamber of Commerce promoted the atomic explosions as if they were tourist attractions. Hotels published schedules and maps of the atomic tests and invited guests out to the mountains to watch the mushroom clouds in the early dawn. The hotels even provided box lunches. Visitors could drive out to Mount Charleston, where they could get a fantastic view of the atomic explosions. The whole city got into the act when bars started serving "atomic cocktails." A Flamingo Hotel hair stylist designed an "atomic hairdo," and the city held "Miss Atomic Bomb" contests.

Operation Ranger was considered a success since no significant levels of radioactivity were detected outside the test area. No one was injured. The site was expanded in 1958, 1961, 1964, and 1967 until it reached its present size of 1,350 square miles. Ground zero was moved twenty miles farther north to Yucca Flat. Eventually 126 tests would take place before above-ground atomic testing was banned in October 1958.

Ichthyosaur Fossils Excavated at Berlin Ghost Town
· 1954 ·

Fossils were first noticed in the Gabbs Valley by early miners in 1869. These miners sent some bones to Philadelphia, where Dr. Joseph Leidy examined them. The fossils were forgotten until some students under Professor John C. Merriam found more in 1904 and 1905. At the time, no one could identify which animal the fossils were from. In 1928, Professor Simon W. Muller of Stanford was exploring the area, and he identified the bones as belonging to the ichthyosaur, an ancient lizardlike fish, but he didn't excavate any fossils. In 1952, Margaret Wheat of Fallon started digging in the Union Canyon area on a very small scale. In 1954, a major excavation by Dr. Charles L. Camp, Dr. Samuel P. Welles, and some high school and college students from the San Francisco area discovered a large accumulation of ichthyosaur remains near the ghost town of Berlin.

Dr. Camp became interested in paleontology and archaeology while growing up in southern California, studying under the naturalist Joseph Grinnell. He had also visited the John C. Merriam fossil beds at Rancho Los Angeles Brea several times. He studied at Throop Academy (California Institute of Technology), the University of California at Berkeley, and Columbia, where he received his doctorate. During his tenure at the University of California, he directed many expeditions. He was also interested in the development of the American West which was how he came to be digging in the Shoshone Mountains near Berlin in 1954.

Dr. Camp's crew first dug on the hillsides above and behind the visible specimens at a location known as Visitor's Quarry. Mudstone lay beneath the fossils while brittle shale lay on top. A six-inch-thick, yellowish-white layer of calcite lay about eight inches above the main layer of fossils. The colors of the layers contrasted so dramatically that the layers could be used to judge how deep the fossils were buried. The calcite coloring allowed the crew to use heavy equipment to remove the upper layers of rock knowing they would not be disturbing any fossils. Then they used hand tools to remove the rest of the rock. After the fossils were removed from their rock matrix, Dr. Camp sandblasted them to expose the bluish color of the limestone that had replaced the original bone.

The fossils discovered on the lowest level were the biggest. These larger specimens had bodies eight feet thick with several flippers. The eye sockets were a foot across, and the tails were twenty-five feet long with a six-foot triangular fin at the end. The vertebrae reached twelve inches in diameter. Based on these measurements, the scientists estimated that the ichthyosaurs weighed forty tons and were sixty feet long. The heads were ten feet long with several rows of cone-shaped teeth and a long pointed snout. Most of the heads were sharply turned to one side, some even doubled back alongside the body. This fact suggested that the ichthyosaurs were still alive and fighting to get free of the mud when they died.

The excavation also uncovered fossils of small burrowing clams, creeping snails, and a shellfish called ammonite. Oddly there is no evidence at this site of any type of fish that the ichthyosaur might have eaten. It is estimated that the ichthyosaur existed for about 135 million years.

How did the ichthyosaurs come to be there? It all started about 200 million years ago, when this part of Nevada and much of the rest of the western American coast lay under the ocean. The land was covered with forests, swamps, and lakes—a vastly different topography than today. Ferns, cycads (small palm-type trees), monkey-puzzle pines, and horsetail plants dwelled on the land at the time of the first ichthyosaur. There were also reptiles similar to crocodiles and salamanders. Mud flats formed along the shore where sediments washed up from the ocean. Ichthyosaurs got trapped in these mud flats when venturing too close to shore and died. The ichthyosaurs decayed, leaving only their skeletons behind. Rivers deposited more mud, silt, and logs on top of the mud flats. The logs, and eventually the bones, became petrified, turning into limestone.

About ten to twenty million years ago, layers of earth's crust slid below others, forcing the top layers up. Mud flats that were once below the surface and further west were now exposed and dozens of miles further east than where they were formed. Below the surface, molten lava formed volcanic cones along the present Cascade Mountains. The ichthyosaur beds were buried again by ash and lava deposits from volcanoes. They were revealed once more when that material eroded away, exposing the fossils.

The scientists discovered ichthyosaur bones on three levels at Visitor's Quarry; most bones were found on the lowest level. At least four large specimens rested on that level, and remains of at least sixteen others were found in the quarry. Remains of about thirty-seven ichthyosaurs were found in the area. Most of the fossils found were adult creatures. Dr. Camp excavated one fossil then refilled some areas to preserve the remaining fossils for future study.

Though the ichthyosaur was found on all the continents except Antarctica, the specimen excavated by Dr. Camp is the only complete skeleton (approximately fifty-five feet long) of this extinct marine reptile. This skeleton was put on permanent display at the University of Nevada at Las Vegas Museum of Natural History.

In 1955, the state set aside 515 acres to establish the Ichthyosaur Paleontological State Monument. It is located near the mouth of West Union Canyon in the Shoshone Mountains about twenty-three miles east of Gabbs. Dr. Camp and his crew explored the area through 1957. In 1966, the State Parks Department and the Forest Service Job Corps Program built an A-frame shelter over Visitor's Quarry to preserve the fossils. Later the dig was fully enclosed in a building.

In 1970, the state acquired the adjacent ghost town of Berlin, so the park was renamed Berlin-Ichthyosaur State Park. The size of the park was increased to 1,127 acres to include the ghost town. Thirteen buildings from Berlin were preserved. The town site was listed on the National Register of Historic Places in 1971.

In 1973, at eighty years old, Dr. Camp returned to the area to dedicate the expanded park. Sculptor William Huff chiseled a life-size, sixty-foot ichthyosaur and Dr. Camp's profile on a ceremonial plaque. The fossil site was designated a Registered Natural Landmark in 1975. In 1977, the state eternally honored the ichthyosaur by adopting it as the official state fossil.

U-2 Tested at Area 51
• 1955 •

Insiders knew it as Watertown. Aircraft and military buffs called it Dreamland after its call sign on the control tower. The rest of America would know it as Area 51. Where is this mysterious place? This dry, desolate area, dominated by a dry lake bed known as Groom Lake, is located in southern Nevada, about sixty-five miles north of Las Vegas.

In 1953, the Cold War was in full force. The Pentagon was worried that Russia might have more weapons and bombs than the United States. Bombers had already been sent over Russia for photo reconnaissance, but they kept getting shot down. Major John Seaberg, an aerospace engineer at Wright-Patterson Air Force Base in Ohio, had an idea that would combine a high-speed jet engine with a wing design capable of reaching seventy thousand feet—far above the range of Russian missiles.

The Central Intelligence Agency (CIA) awarded a contract to design the plane to an aerospace company called Lockheed. The Skunkworks division of Lockheed in southern California worked twelve hour days, six days a week, for several months to build the jet. The director of Skunkworks, Kelly Johnson, was in charge of the project. Engineers had to lengthen the traditional fuselage to accommodate the engine. So the fuselage would be lighter, they pounded out the aluminum skin until it was only two one-hundredths of an inch thick. To trim additional weight, the plane would have no ejection seat; if a pilot had to get out of the plane, he would have to climb out. The engine was designed to use a special type of fuel that would not freeze at seventy thousand feet. They called the new plane "U-2."

By 1955, the plane was ready for testing. Usually the Air Force tested high speed aircraft at Edwards Air Force Base, but that base was not considered secure enough for U-2 testing. Not only did the CIA not want Russia to know what it was doing, it also wanted to hide its mission from the American public as long as possible. Lockheed chief test pilot Tony LeVier recommended a dry lake bed called Groom Lake in southern Nevada as the testing site. Besides its hard surface, the site was miles from anything. People would stay away because of the danger of radioactive fallout from the nearby Nevada Test Site. Since Groom Lake was close to the Test Site, the area was already secure.

Lockheed flew the pieces of the first prototype to Groom Lake on July 24, 1955. After reassembly, the first taxi test took place on August 1. Pilot LeVier steered the plane while he took it up to fifty knots. When he tried to stop, the brakes wouldn't work, and he had to coast to a stop. He tried it again, speeding along at seventy knots, kicking up a large cloud of dust that obscured the officials' view of the plane. They did not see that the plane had actually left the ground, unbeknownst even to LeVier. Usually a plane had to taxi up to one hundred knots to take off. But because the U-2 was so light, it only needed sixty knots for liftoff.

The first real flight test took place on August 4, 1955. Several problems delayed the takeoff, but the test finally continued. LeVier flew the plane up to eight thousand feet. It started to rain, so LeVier had to end the test early. Rain was always a serious concern, because the lake bed could turn into muck when it was wet. But LeVier ran into another problem. To save weight, the U-2 had been designed with landing gear on only the nose and the tail, instead of on each wing and the nose as usual. Pogo sticks supported the wings during takeoff but dropped off as the plane left the ground. There was nothing to support the wings when landing, so landing on the two wheels would be tricky.

Johnson and LeVier disagreed on how the landing should be attempted. Johnson insisted that the plane be landed nose first.

LeVier thought the plane should be landed on both wheels at the same time, but he tried it Johnson's way first. As soon as the nose wheel touched the ground, the plane began to porpoise—a serious condition in which a plane can bounce itself apart. LeVier took off again. He tried the nose landing again but with the same results. Finally he landed on both wheels and got down with no problem, though there was still a small amount of bounce.

LeVier flew twenty more test missions in the prototype, including the first flight to sixty thousand feet. After that, the U-2 was ready for vigorous testing in a production model. The CIA ordered a whole fleet of U-2s, which were built in Oildale, California, during 1956–57. They were shipped in pieces by truck to Nevada. The trucks traveled at night so the drivers couldn't see exactly where they were going. The planes were reassembled in Nevada and the testing began.

Twenty-nine top pilots from the Air Force were chosen to participate in the tests. None of them knew what their mission was; they just knew it was so secret they were all given aliases. Three groups of pilots flew test missions, flying two or three flights a week in the new spy planes.

The production model was very fragile and could stall out or vibrate apart. Several pilots crashed and died during this test period. One pilot died when flying at night; he crashed into a telephone pole when blinded by lights at the end of the runway. Another pilot crashed while trying to shake loose the pogo sticks. His erratic flying, combined with the weight of the fuel, caused the plane to stall and crash.

The first U-2 flew over Russia on July 4, 1956. The Russians detected the plane right away but were unable to shoot it down. Realizing that the plane's eighty-foot wings were easily detected on radar, officials decided to cover the U-2's belly with a metallic grid and special paint to absorb radar waves. This scheme did help hide the plane from radar waves but also caused the engine to heat up and the hydraulic pumps to fail. A test pilot had to bail out of his plane when the engine quit because it got too hot. Because there was no ejection seat he had to climb out. Once he was out, he was hit by the tail of the plane and killed.

There would be nine more fatal accidents during test flights and training—all before Americans learned that the U-2 existed. When Francis Gary Powers crashed in the Soviet Union in May of 1960, it was the last time a U-2 would fly over Russia. But the plane would be used for other missions. It discovered missiles in Cuba in 1962, and it was used during the Persian Gulf War in 1992.

The Strange Wedding of Elvis Presley
· 1967 ·

Many celebrities have been married in Las Vegas over the years. Nelson Eddy, Artie Shaw, Bela Lugosi, Mary Martin, and Bette Midler were all married there. But one of the most celebrated and one of the strangest weddings to take place in Las Vegas was that of Elvis Presley and Priscilla Beaulieu.

Elvis was living at Graceland when his prospective father-in-law, Major Beaulieu, asked him when he was going to a set a date for his wedding. Elvis decided that the wedding would be during the holidays. However, Elvis didn't propose to Priscilla until Christmas Eve, 1966, and even then didn't set a date. Beaulieu and Elvis's manager, Tom Parker, began to pressure Elvis. Beaulieu wanted Elvis to make Priscilla "legitimate." After all, she and Elvis had been living together for five years. Parker noticed that Elvis's music and movies weren't quite as popular as they had previously been. He figured Elvis's wedding would regenerate interest. On March 15, 1967, Elvis's good friends Jerry and Sandy West got married in Las Vegas. It was after that that Elvis said he would get married after the filming of *Clambake*—about the end of April.

From there, Parker took over, and everyone began to refer to the upcoming event as "the Colonel's wedding." Just two days before the wedding, Parker called his good friend Milton Prell, who had recently purchased the Aladdin Hotel in Las Vegas. He wanted Prell to host the wedding. Having the wedding in Las Vegas would give Parker an excuse for not inviting part of Elvis's entourage that he felt had too much influence over Elvis. He also figured he could dodge the press more easily there and release the news of Elvis's wedding under his own terms.

On April 29, 1967, Parker announced it was time. Elvis, Priscilla, and their families and friends gathered in Palm Springs. But the press learned of Elvis's arrival and the town was soon mobbed. In the early morning of May 1, Elvis and Priscilla flew with friends George Klein and Joe and Joanie Esposito to Las Vegas on Frank Sinatra's Learjet. At four o'clock in the morning a limousine drove them to the Clark County clerk's office to get a marriage license. Elvis didn't carry cash, so Joe Esposito paid the fifteen-dollar fee.

The wedding party gathered at the Aladdin. Elvis talked to the official, a Jewish judge named David Zenoff, Parker's personal friend. Zenoff was impressed with Elvis's modesty and respect. He also met Priscilla, who was so nervous she couldn't talk. She just nodded her head when Zenoff explained how the ceremony would proceed.

Meanwhile, Elvis's friends and family got ready for the ceremony. Just a few minutes before the ceremony, many of Elvis's friends found out that they would not be allowed to attend the wedding, which was to be held in Milton Prell's private suite at the Aladdin. The suite was not very large, only accommodating seventeen people. A long time friend, Red West, got impatient for the ceremony to start so he asked Joe Esposito, co-best man with Marty Lacker, if he knew what was going on. Esposito told him that Parker had excluded West, as well as several others, from the ceremony so as to not show favoritism. West was furious. He was especially upset because Elvis had been his own best man. He walked out and refused to even attend the reception. The others resented the slight too, though not to the degree that West did. Most blamed it on Parker and not on Elvis.

When the ceremony was about to begin, everyone took their places. The suite was decorated with twenty-five towering candles and dozens of flowers. Elvis and Priscilla stood in front of

Zenoff. Elvis wore a black paisley brocade tuxedo and combed his hair into a huge pompadour that had been built up over a wire pouf. He wore cowboy boots and heavy makeup. Priscilla wore a traditional white gown but she also had on heavy black eye makeup and her hair was dyed black. She did not have time to be fitted for a tailored gown, so her gown was "off the rack." The guests, many of them the Colonel's staff and colleagues, gathered around the bride and groom. Priscilla's thirteen-year-old sister was the maid of honor. George Klein and cousins Patsy Presley and Billy Smith were there. For some reason Elvis's jeweler, Harry Levitch, was there. Parker had invited two MGM photographers to the wedding. He told them where to stand and to remain there throughout the entire ceremony. During the ceremony, one of the photographers had difficulty getting a good shot. When he moved slightly to get a better angle, Parker rapped the photographer over the head with his cane.

The ceremony itself was unmemorable and over in eight minutes. Immediately after the ceremony, Parker rushed the Presleys straight to a press conference near the hotel pool. Then Parker led the way to the reception.

At the reception, Parker laid out a sumptuous party. There was a six-tier wedding cake iced with roses, pearls, and 1,600 sugar rosettes. The hotel served ham and eggs, southern fried chicken, roast suckling pig, fresh poached candy salmon, eggs Minette, oysters Rockefeller, and champagne. A string ensemble performed romantic ballads including *Love Me Tender*. A strolling accordionist also played. Redd Foxx was one of the guests. Executives from MGM, William Morris, and RCA were also there. Some family members stayed for the reception, but some of Elvis's closest friends chose not to attend.

Elvis and Priscilla did not get to plan their honeymoon either. Parker quickly flew them back to Palm Springs to ensure that Elvis finished making his film *Clambake*. After all, Parker was collecting fifty percent of Elvis's earnings as his fee! When the filming was over, Elvis toyed with the idea of taking Priscilla to Europe, but

Parker vetoed that idea, claiming that Elvis's European fans would hound him about performing there. The Presleys went to the Bahamas instead, but did not enjoy their trip and came home early.

Elvis returned to Las Vegas many times and was one of the top performers there during the rest of his lifetime. It's hard to visit Las Vegas without noticing the influence that Elvis still has in the city. Businesses all over town claim "Elvis was here." Many couples choose an "Elvis" theme for their own weddings. A show called "Legends in Concert" features imitators of many famous entertainers, alive and dead. The Elvis impersonators always bring down the house. There are hundreds of Elvis Presley impersonators around the world that belong to the Elvis Presley Impersonators International Association. They get together every year for a convention at the Imperial Palace in Las Vegas.

Challenging the Landspeed Record
· 1997 ·

Most people are aware that the Bonneville Salt Flats in western Utah have long been used as a place for racing and setting speed records. Ever since 1906, when a Stanley steampowered car set a speed record of 127.659 miles per hour, others have tried to go faster. An Englishman named Richard Noble set a landspeed record of 633.468 miles per hour at the Black Rock Desert on October 4, 1983. Several times since then, racers have tried to beat that mark.

In 1997, two racers came back to the Black Rock Desert to try to beat the record. In addition, they would attempt to break the sound barrier, which at four thousand feet above sea level would be about 765 miles per hour. One racer was Craig Breedlove, an American who had held the record at five different times between 1963 and 1965. In the process, he became the first person to travel over four hundred, five hundred, and six hundred miles per hour on land. For the 1997 run, he brought his jet-powered "Spirit of America" vehicle, newly repaired from damage sustained in a record-breaking attempt the year before. The other racer was Andy Green, a retired Royal Air Force pilot who would drive Richard Noble's Thrust SSC (Super Sonic Car). Noble and Green wanted to keep the record for the British.

The racers and their crews prepared for the record-setting event after the first of September. Part of the preparation consisted of obtaining permits from the Bureau of Land Management to race in the Black Rock Desert. Noble and Green tuned up the two fifty-thousand-horsepower Rolls-Royce Spey 205 engines installed in the Thrust SSC. Breedlove tuned up his super-compact General Electric forty-five-thousand-horsepower J79 jet-engine-powered car. When the competitors arrived at the Black Rock Desert, the course was prepared. Crew members marked ten different tracks across the desert. Pebbles and other debris were manually removed so that nothing could be sucked into the intakes of the jet-propelled cars.

Who would win? The record could only be set after the driver completed two runs. The average of both runs would be calculated to see if a record-setting speed had been reached. The second run had to take place within an hour of the first one for the record to count.

On September 8, 1997, the two men went at it for the first time. Green didn't even reach 150 miles per hour before his car developed battery problems. The problem led to a drop in hydraulic pressure, and the car had to be towed back to base. Breedlove's "Spirit of America" reached 324 miles per hour before it developed engine problems when something got sucked into the intake pipes. The "something" was later discovered to be a bolt. It wiped out several compressor blades, in addition to causing other damage. The car was shipped back to Rio Vista, California to receive a new engine.

The two crews were back out by September 20, but more technical problems haunted them. Green had to end his run after reaching four hundred miles per hour when his onboard computer shut down. Breedlove stopped his car after reaching 313 miles per hour because the car's rear end felt wobbly.

On September 23, Green made another run at the record. Breedlove did not run that day, since he was still working on a malfunctioning fuel pump and faulty wheel bearings. Conditions seemed perfect for Green when he got the Thrust SSC up to an amazing 719.137 miles per hour! But the dual parachutes that slow the car failed, and Green had to hit the brakes at two hundred miles per hour. This caused him to overshoot the end of the thirteen-mile course by 1.4 miles. Because of that, he could not make the required second run. After the run was over, Noble and Green found that the car's brakes had heated up to 1,472 degrees Fahrenheit.

But the goal was in sight. On September 25, Green made another try. This time he was successful! He reached 700.661 miles per hour on the first dash, turned around, and reached 728.008 miles per hour on the second trip. His average speed between the two runs was 714.144, demolishing his previous record of 633.47 miles per hour! But Noble and Green weren't through; they still wanted to break the sound barrier.

On October 3, Green made his first attempt at the sound barrier. Green had to adjust the tailfin after a test run. But when he got ready to go, too much headwind made the attempt too dangerous. Breedlove did not run that day. Three more days of heavy winds prevented any racing at all.

On October 6, the winds were finally calm and both teams were ready to go. Green reached 714.427 miles per hour in one direction and 727.86 miles per hour on the return trip. The average was higher than his record setting run on September 25, but this run didn't count because he did not make his second run within the one hour allotted. Meanwhile, Breedlove reached 531 miles per hour, the fastest run he had made all year.

Green's next attempt was delayed because rain, snow, and hail made the desert surface very slippery. On October 13, the weather finally cleared enough for Green to make another run at breaking the sound barrier. And he did it! Green reached 764.168 miles per hour on the first trip and 760.125 miles per hour on the second run. Spectators heard the sonic boom and saw the shock wave at the nose of the car. But Green had trouble with his parachutes, and he overshot the end of the course by one and a half miles. It took him sixty-one minutes to turn the car around and make the second run. He was too late by one minute.

But now Green knew he could do it. So on October 15, he

tried again, and this time he reached a speed of 759.333 miles per hour in the first run and 766.609 miles per hour in the second run. To put this in perspective, the car would have easily beat a Boeing 737! The United States Automobile Club timed the event, calculating an average speed of 763.035 miles per hour, or Mach 1.02—two percent faster than the speed of sound! The date was fifty years and one day after Chuck Yeager became the first pilot to fly faster than the speed of sound.

Nevada is now becoming known as a car-racing mecca. The new Las Vegas International Motor Speedway hosts stock car, motorcross, and truck races. Highway 318 between Lund and Hiko hosts the country's only open-road auto race. And the Black Rock Desert will continue to be the destination for future racers who want to challenge the landspeed record.

The Las Vegas Flood
· 1999 ·

Early on the morning of July 8, 1999, ominous thunderheads built up in Clark County, Nevada. Fast-moving air collided with moisture blown up from Mexico and the Gulf of California. It was only a matter of time before the cloudburst. The one-hundred-year storm began about 10:30 A.M.

The worst part of the storm lasted from 10:30 A.M. to 4:30 P.M. In this part of the state, rain seldom tops four inches a year, yet in just a few hours, some areas received close to their annual allotment! McCarran International Airport measured 1.29 inches. Blue Diamond, a few miles west of Las Vegas received an incredible 3.19 inches of rain, most of which came down between 11 A.M. and 12:15 P.M.!

Las Vegas was brought to a standstill. During the flood, firefighters responded to a huge number of trouble calls ranging from stalled cars to collapsed roofs. Some houses had been struck by lightning. Flood waters engulfed major intersections, snarling traffic and stranding motorists. Fire trucks and police helicopters rescued people from the roofs of their cars when high water set their cars afloat. Twenty flights were delayed as much as forty-five minutes. Air traffic controllers diverted two flights to Los Angeles and one flight to Phoenix. Mud slides and rock slides covered the Summerlin Parkway northwest of the city. Though they had not suffered any damage, Wells Fargo Bank closed its sixty branches in the Las Vegas area to allow workers to get home. The Meadows Mall and the Boulevard Mall also closed early to allow their employees to get home.

There were no major problems with utilities, although about 2,500 residents were temporarily without electricity. About six hundred customers lost their Sprint telephone service for a short time. Sunrise Hospital lost ninety-five percent of its phone service when lightning struck one of the phone lines. The North Las Vegas Airport lost power and closed its radio tower for the day.

Las Vegas's renowned entertainment was greatly diminished that evening, as many of the performers canceled their shows. Magician Rick Thomas missed his afternoon show at the Tropicana. Magician Lance Burton canceled his evening show at the Monte Carlo. Magician Steve Wyrick canceled his evening shows at the Lady Luck. Musician Peter Frampton rescheduled his performance at the Mandalay Bay for August.

Many hotels also closed some of their attractions as a safety precaution. The Imperial Palace canceled its outdoor luau. The Tropicana canceled its weekly Miss Hawaiian Tropic pageant. The MGM Grand closed its pool and Grand Adventures theme park. The New York New York closed its Manhattan Express roller coaster. The Stratosphere closed its tower.

The next day residents assessed the damage. Water damage affected businessmen and homeowners alike. Lucky's Grocery Store had roof damage due to the heavy rain. So did the Family Fitness Center and the Harley Davidson dealership. Other stores and businesses remained intact but developed leaks in their roofs. The leaky roof of Mountain View Hospital necessitated moving several patients. The facility also shut down the surgical and birthing units due to potential electrical problems.

The only major Strip casino to suffer damage was Caesars Palace, which received damage to one sixteen-table pit area in the casino and to several stores in the Forum Shops. Water flowed through a back service entrance into the shops and all the way into the casino. The Imperial Palace Casino closed a 570-space parking garage for several hours when water from the Flamingo Wash, one of the primary drainage ditches in Las Vegas, pooled into a three-foot-deep lake. The Golden Nugget, a downtown casino, sustained damage to its south lobby and casino bar. Flood waters caused damage to one convention area at the Las Vegas Convention Center. Several golf courses were damaged, especially the Tournament Players Club at Summerlin which lost a thirty-foot section of cart path that was torn out by flood waters and floated two hundred yards away. High water also washed out several bunkers and uprooted several small trees.

One of the areas most affected by the flood was the Miracle Mile Mobile Home Park, a 540-home residential area just off the Boulder Highway. Mud flowed onto the park's streets. Tree branches, garbage, and rocks were swept into the park. Some homes slid off into the wash when flood waters undercut their foundations. Trash cans, barbecues, a huge tree, a car, huge concrete blocks, crayfishes, and toads floated through the park. The Red Cross immediately opened an emergency shelter at the Woodbury Middle School for displaced residents.

What makes this area so susceptible to floods? Las Vegas is situated at the bottom of a bowl right in the path of several natural washes. Most of the year, these washes are either totally dry or carry just small amounts of water. But the soil in the area is so shallow that it does not absorb water. During a flash flood like this one, the washes become torrents as flood waters seek their way to Lake Mead, the lowest point in the area. The Flamingo and Las Vegas Washes become orange rivers in comparison to their usual trickle.

Though destructive, the 1999 storm was not one of the worst in history. Other notable storms dumped much more water in the area and caused more damage. One of the worst storms occurred in September 1974, when a twelve-foot wall of water swept through Eldorado Canyon, fifty miles south of Las Vegas, destroying everything in its path, including a marina, a restaurant, a gasoline dock, boats, fifty cars, and twenty mobile homes.

During the last few years, the county has been working on ways to protect itself from future floods. Las Vegas began work on a system of catch basins that will collect excess runoff before it floods low-lying areas of the county. Only two of these basins were completed when the 1999 storm hit Las Vegas, but the damage could have been much worse had the basins not been there. One of the basins saved a nearby nursing home and a center for mentally disabled people from serious damage. Only two deaths were blamed on the flood. A woman died in a weather-related car accident, and a man was found dead in the Flamingo Wash after the storm.

The county requested assistance from the Federal Emergency Management Agency. Damage was initially estimated at thirteen million dollars then later raised to over twenty million dollars. At least five million dollars of the estimate included damages to the flood control system. Other estimated damage included commercial property, residential property, a portion of the Boulder Highway, and numerous roads and sidewalks. Approximately one hundred homes sustained major damage and at least three hundred needed minor repairs. Federal assistance was granted for seventy-five percent of the total damage, and state and local sources covered the balance.

A Potpourri of Nevada Facts

- Nevada is America's seventh largest state with 110,540 square miles. It measures 485 miles from north to south and 315 miles east to west at its widest point. Eighty-six percent of the land is federally controlled.

- Nevada means "snow-capped" in Spanish.

- Nevada has three nicknames: the Sagebrush State, the Silver State, and the Battle Born State. It is usually referred to as the Silver State.

- Nevada's state colors are silver and blue.

- In 1864, President Abraham Lincoln admitted Nevada to the Union as the thirty-sixth state.

- Every year, on October 31, Nevada celebrates its formation as a state. It is one of only two states to annually celebrate its admission into the union.

- In 1998, the estimated population of Nevada was 1,852,650, making it the thirty-ninth most populous state. Nevada's most populous city is Las Vegas with an estimated 441,230 people. The estimated population of Carson City, the capital, is 51,860.

- The state animal is the desert bighorn sheep. It can survive in Nevada because it can tolerate long periods without water. About 1,500 desert bighorn sheep live on Nevada's Desert Wildlife Refuge, more than any other place in the world.

- The state song is called "Home Means Nevada." It was written by Bertha Raffeto of Reno. The state adopted the song in 1933.

- The state precious stone is the black fire opal. The Virgin Valley in northern Nevada is the only place in North America where this stone is found in any significant quantity.

- The state bird is the mountain bluebird.

- One of the state trees is the bristlecone pine. In Nevada, some of these trees are over 4,000 years old, making them the oldest living things on Earth. Bristlecone pines generally grow between fifteen and thirty feet high. The diameter continues to grow even after the tree has reached full height, resulting in massive trunks. The other state tree is the single-leaf pinon.

- Laughlin is the state's hottest spot and the country's second hottest spot. The record high temperature was 125 degrees Fahrenheit on June 29, 1994.

- Nevada is the driest state in the country, receiving an average of only 7 inches of rain per year.

- Only 1.4% of Nevada is under cultivation, mostly in hay and forage crops.

- The Humboldt River is the longest river in the state. It flows 500 miles from north of Wells to the Humboldt Sink, southwest of Lovelock. It is also the longest river in the shortest amount of space in North America.

- Nevada ranks first in gold production, producing $2.7 billion or 7.7 million troy ounces in 1996. That amount was 66% of the total U.S. production. Carlin is the site of the world's largest gold mine.

- Nevada also ranks first in silver production, with 20.5 million troy ounces produced in 1996. That amount was about 35% of the total U.S. production.

- Nevada is America's most mountainous state with 150 mountain ranges. Boundary Peak, in the White Mountain Range, is the highest peak in Nevada at 13,143 feet.

- The lowest point in Nevada is at the Colorado River in Clark County at 470 feet.

- Nevada has about 28,000 wild horses. This is about 70% of the horses thought to be wild in the United States.

- Nye County is Nevada's largest county with 18,294 square miles. It is the third largest county in the country.

- Winnemucca has the largest potato field in the United States and the largest potato dehydration plant in the world. Winnemucca Farms Inc. ships over 180,000 pounds of potatoes per year, some of which are made into Pringles potato chips.

- The small town of Pahrump gets less than four inches of rain per year, but it has a large underground supply. The town sits on top of the third largest aquifer in the United States.

- The world's tallest roller coaster is the Desperado at Buffalo Bill's Resort in Jean. The roller coaster has a vertical drop of 225 feet. It speeds along at over 80 miles per hour.

- Lake Tahoe Facts: The lake sits at 6,229 feet above sea level. It is 22 miles long by 12 miles wide. It has 71 miles of shoreline. It contains 122,160,280 acre-feet of water. Its average depth is 989 feet, with its deepest point at 1,645 feet. The surface water temperature averages 68 degrees Fahrenheit maximum and 41 degrees Fahrenheit minimum. The average annual snowfall at the lake is 216 inches.

- Gambling and tourism in Las Vegas generate more annual revenue than any other business in the state. Only the U.S. Mint generates money faster.

- The Stratosphere Tower in Las Vegas is 1,149 feet high. It is the tallest building west of the Mississippi and the tallest free-standing observation tower in the United States. It weighs more than 100 million pounds and has 290 miles of rebar.

- The world's tallest freestanding sign is at the Las Vegas Hilton. The sign is twenty stories high (279 feet), 164 feet wide, and has over 6 miles of neon and fluorescent lights. It cost $9 million to build. The total surface area of the sign is 70,100 square feet.

- The "Lucky the Clown" sign outside the Circus Circus Hotel and Casino in Las Vegas was built in 1968. The 120-foot-high sign cost $1 million. The entire hotel cost only $15 million to build.

- Four million meals are served each year at the Circus Circus Casino buffet, making it the busiest restaurant in the world.

- In 1993, when the new MGM Grand Hotel and Casino opened, it was the largest hotel on earth. It has 5,005 rooms, serviced by 97 elevators. It took thirty-nine armored cars two nights to deliver the 3.5 million quarters necessary to run the casino. The casino covers 171,000 square feet. There are also 10 restaurants, a convention center, and an amusement park on the grounds.

- The Venetian Hotel has a 1.7-million-square-foot convention center, the world's largest private hotel convention facility under one roof.

- The Luxor's pyramid-shaped hotel has 30 stories made of 26,783 glass plates. The beacon at the tip of the pyramid is the brightest beacon in the world, shining with 40 billion candle-power. The beacon is visible to planes 250 miles away in Los

Angeles. The Luxor's atrium in the middle of the pyramid is the largest in the world, topping out at 29 million cubic feet. It is large enough to hold nine Boeing 747s stacked one on top of the other.

- When the Las Vegas Motor Speedway was built in 1996, it was the largest excavation in the state. It is the only major Super Speedway in the world that has an Interstate off-ramp that leads directly into its parking lot. It contains enough steel to stretch from Las Vegas to New York and back—about 10 million linear feet. It contains 600,000 tons of concrete. There are 42,000 tons of asphalt coating the racing surfaces, equal to 17 miles of residential street. The speedway's water tower holds 1,000,000 gallons of water. The first race to be held there, the NASCAR Winston Cup Las Vegas 400, was the largest spectator event in the history of Nevada.

- The first legal prize fight in the United States was held in Carson City on March 17, 1897. It was also the first world championship fight and the first prize fight to be filmed. Bob Fitzsimmons beat the reigning champion, "Gentleman Jim" Corbett, in the fourteenth round.

- Movies that have been totally or partially filmed in Nevada are *An Innocent Man, The Shootist, The Greatest Story Ever Told, Total Recall, Top Gun, Rain Man, Misery, The Professionals, Over the Top, The Misfits, Melvin & Howard, Rocky IV, Pink Cadillac, Sister Act,* and *Independence Day.*

- Lahontan Dam, near Fallon, was part of the first ever federal reclamation project. The Newlands Water Project was approved in 1902. The earthen dam, 120 feet high and 1,300 feet wide, was finished in 1914.

- American Flat was once the site of the world's largest cyanide plant.

- The Pershing County Courthouse in Lovelock is one of only two round courthouses in the country. It was built in 1921.

- In the mid-1800s George Washington Gale Ferris imported trees from the East Coast and planted them throughout Carson City. In 1937, the Colorado blue spruce he planted was designated Nevada's official Christmas tree. His son later invented the Ferris Wheel.

- The Pyramid Lake Reservation is the oldest Indian reservation in the United States, set aside in 1859. It was legally recognized by the government in 1874.

- Pyramid Lake is the largest natural lake in the state at 27 miles long and 9 miles wide.

- Nevada was the site of the world's first execution by lethal gas. The criminal was a murderer named Gee Jon, who was executed in Carson City in 1924.

- The Lake Mead reservoir, impounded behind Hoover Dam, is 225 square miles, with 550 miles of shoreline. It is 500 feet deep at its deepest points. It is the largest body of water impounded by a dam (30,500,000 acre-feet) and the largest manmade lake in the United States.

- At completion, Hoover Dam was 726 feet high and 66 stories wide at its base. It required 4.5 million cubic yards of concrete, enough for a twenty-foot highway from San Francisco to New York City. The dam cost $165 million, all of which was repaid by the sale of electricity. The largest cableway in the world was built at Hoover Dam during its construction, and it is still in use today. It has a 150-ton capacity and allowed men, equipment, and concrete to be hauled across the canyon or to the canyon floor below.

- The Basic Magnesium Plant was the largest refractory in the world when it was completed in 1943. The plant was built with 20,000,000 bricks, including 18,500,500 acid bricks and 1,500,000 fire bricks. Other big numbers associated in the construction of the plant: 305 miles of pipe, 355 fire hydrants, $12 million worth of silver used for the electrolytic cells (copper was scarce at the time), 2,525 tons of cement, and 18 miles of standard gauge railroad track inside the plant.

Bibliography

Associated Press. "Speed record targeted." *Las Vegas Review-Journal,* May 4, 1997.

Associated Press. "Permits sought for record speed try." *Las Vegas Review-Journal*, August 8, 1997.

Associated Press (Tom Gardner). "Speeding ticket to record." *Las Vegas Review-Journal*, September 9, 1997.

Associated Press. "Technical problems plaguing run to set land speed records." *Las Vegas Review-Journal*, September 21, 1997.

Associated Press. "Car goes over 700 mph but does not set record." *Las Vegas Review-Journal*, September 24, 1997.

Associated Press (Martin Griffith). "Racing to a world record." *Las Vegas Review-Journal*, September 26, 1997.

Associated Press. "Wind, woes thwart attempt." *Las Vegas Review-Journal*, October 4, 1997.

Associated Press. "Land speed duel races to fastest times for both teams." *Las Vegas Review-Journal*, October 7, 1997.

Associated Press. "British team breaks sound barrier." *Las Vegas Review-Journal*, October 14, 1997.

Associated Press. "OPINION: A marvel of technology." *Las Vegas Review-Journal*, October 20, 1997.

Associated Press. "Sense of history drove team to record." *Las Vegas Review-Journal*, October 23, 1997.

Associated Press (Angie Wagner). "Heavy rains turn streets into rivers, strand motorists." *Las Vegas Review-Journal*, July 8, 1999.

Bach, Lisa and Natalie Patton. "Miracle Mile Mobile Home Park goes from quiet to chaotic." *Las Vegas Review-Journal*, July 9, 1999.

Ball, Howard. *Justice Downwind: America's Atomic Testing Program in the 1950s*. New York: Oxford University Press, 1986.

Basic Bombardier, Volume 1, No. 45, May 21, 1943 (Basic Magnesium company newsletter).

Bass, Debra D. "Mobile home residents begin cleanup amid shock of damage." *Las Vegas Review-Journal*, July 10, 1999.

Beebe, Lucius, and Charles Clegg. *U.S. West: The Saga of Wells Fargo*. New York: E.P. Dutton & Company, Inc., 1949.

Bendinskis, George. *Pioche Nevada—Nation's Liveliest Ghost Town*. Pioche, NV: Ghost Town Gazette, Fall 1996.

Berg, Andrew D., and Pamela Wolfe. *A&E Biography: Bugsy Siegel, Gambling on the Mob*. Produced by Tower Productions Inc. for A&E Television Networks, New York, 1995.

Berk, Lee. "Winnemucca's Bank Robbery: Cassidy Didn't Do It." *Humboldt Historian*. Volume V, Issue 4. Winnemucca: North Central Nevada Historical Society, Fall 1982.

Berns, Dave and Monica Caruso. "Forum Shops, casino pit at Caesars close." *Las Vegas Review-Journal*, July 9, 1999.

Betenson, Lula Parker, as told to Dora Flack. *Butch Cassidy, My Brother*. Provo: Brigham Young University Press, 1975.

Block, Eugene B. *Great Train Robberies of the West*. New York: Coward-McCann Inc., 1959.

Brown, Peter Harry and Pat H. Brooks. *Down at the End of Lonely Street: The Life and Death of Elvis Presley*. New York: Penguin, Putnam Inc., 1997.

Camp, Charles L. *Child of the Rocks: The Story of Berlin-Ichthyosaur State Park*. Reno: Nevada Bureau of Mines and Geology, 1981.

Castleman, Deke. "Gaming's Grandissimos." *Nevada Magazine*, March/April, 1999.

Darlington, David. *Area 51, The Dreamland Chronicles*. New York: Owl Books, Henry Holt and Co., Inc., 1997.

Darlington, David. *The Mojave: A Portrait of the Definitive American Desert*. New York: Henry Holt and Co., Inc., 1996.

DeNevi, Don. *Western Train Robberies*. Millbrae, CA: Celestial Arts, 1976.

DeQuille, Dan. *The Big Bonanza*. New York: Alfred A. Knopf, Co., 1947.

Drago, Harry Sinclair. *Road Agents and Train Robbers, Half a Century of Western Banditry*. New York: Dodd, Mead, & Company, 1973.

Earl, Phillip I. "Hollywood Comes to the Black Rock: The Story of the Making of *The Winning of Barbara Worth*." *Humboldt Historian*. Winnemucca: North Central Nevada Historical Society, Winter-Spring, 1988.

Earl, Phillip I. "The Disappearance of Roy Frisch." Carson City: *Nevada Magazine*, July/August 1998.

Earl, Phillip I. *This Was Nevada*. Reno: Nevada Historical Society, 1986.

Edwards, John G. "Wells Fargo closes branches; other banks, utilities have few problems." *Las Vegas Review-Journal*, July 9, 1999.

Egan, Ferol. *Sand in a Whirlwind: The Paiute Indian War of 1860*. New York: Doubleday & Company, Inc., 1972.

Elliot, Russell R. *History of Nevada*. Lincoln: University of Nebraska, 1973.

Fenstermaker Danner, Ruth. *Gabbs Valley, Nevada: Its History & Legend*. Winnemucca: Ruth Danner Publisher, 1992.

Folgate, Toddy. "Earthquake, 1915." *Humboldt Historian*. Winnemucca: North Central Nevada Historical Society, Summer-Fall, 1987.

Frady, Steven R. *Red Shirts and Leather Helmets: Volunteer Fire Fighting on the Comstock*. Reno: University of Nevada Press, 1984.

Friess, Steve and Joe Schoenmann. "Officials firm up flood loss estimate." *Las Vegas Review-Journal*, July 13, 1999.

Franks, Michael. "Mark Twain and the *Territorial Enterprise*." *Territorial Enterprise*, http://www.territorial-enterprise.com/tee.htm, 1999.

Gilbert, Bil. *Westering Man, The Life of Joseph Walker*. Norman, OK: University of Oklahoma Press, 1983.

Goldman, Albert. *Elvis*. New York: McGraw-Hill Company, 1981.

Guralnick, Peter. *The Unmaking of Elvis Presley: Careless Love*. Boston: Little, Brown, and Company, 1999.

Hillyer, Katharine. *Young Reporter, Mark Twain, in Virginia City*. Sparks, NV: Western Printing & Publishing Company, 1964.

Hopkins, A.D. *"Howard Eells (1893-1978): Henderson Founder Endured It All." Las Vegas Review-Journal*, http://www.1st100.com/part2/eells.html, May 1999.

Hopkins, A.D. "Magnesium Maggie, Ready to do the Job." *Las Vegas Review-Journal*, http://www.1st100.com/part2/maggie.html, May 1999.

Hopkins, A. D., "Morgan Courtney, Gunfighter from Pioche." *Ghost Town Gazette*. Pioche, NV: Fall 1996.

Horan, James D. *The Outlaws.* Avenel, NJ: Gramercy Press, 1995.

Hulse, James W. *The Nevada Adventure: A History.* Reno: University of Nevada Press, 1966.

Iole, Kevin. "Rains hit several golf courses hard; other facilities OK." *Las Vegas Review-Journal,* July 9, 1999.

Kelley, Charles. *The Outlaw Trail: A History of Butch Cassidy and his Wild Bunch.* Lincoln: University of Nebraska, 1996 (originally published 1959).

Land, Barbara and Myrick. *A Short History of Reno.* Reno: University of Nevada Press, 1995.

Las Vegas Motor Speedway, http://www.lvms.com.

Las Vegas On-Line, "History of Las Vegas." http://www.lvol.com/lvoleg/hist/lvhist.html.

Leckey, Brian, Director. *Extreme Machines: Landspeed Record 3.* Pioneer Productions, produced for the Discovery Channel, 1999.

Leonard, Zenas. *Adventures of a Mountain Man: The Narrative of Zenas Leonard.* Lincoln: University of Nebraska Press, 1978.

Lewis, Oscar. *The Town That Died Laughing: The Story of Austin, Nevada, Rambunctious Early-Day Mining Camp, and of its Reknowned Newspaper, The Reese River Reveille.* Boston: Little, Brown and Company, 1955.

Lillard, Richard G. *A Desert Challenge: An Interpretation of Nevada.* New York: Alfred A. Knopf Company, 1942.

Macy, Robert. "After 50 Years, Siegel Legend Haunts Resort." Las Vegas: *Las Vegas SUN,* Inc., December 20, 1996. http://www.lasvegassun.com/sunbin/stories/text/1996/dec/20/505410502.html.

Mason, Dorothy. *The Pony Express in Nevada.* Carson City, NV: Nevada State Museum, 1996.

Mathias, Donald E. and Valerie S. Berry. *A Place Called Jarbidge*. Glendora, CA: Donald E. Mathias and Valerie S. Berry, 1997.

McGlashan, C. F. *History of the Donner Party: A Tragedy of the Sierra*. Stanford: Stanford University Press, 1995, originally published 1880, San Francisco: A. L. Brancroft & Co., Printers.

McLaughlin, Mark. *Sierra Stories—True Tales of Tahoe*. Carnelian Bay, CA.: MicMac Publishing, 1997.

Miller, B. F. *Nevada in the Making*. Reno: Nevada State Historical Society Papers, Volume IV, 1923-1924.

Miller, Richard L. *Under the Cloud: The Decades of Nuclear Testing*. New York: The Free Press, A Division of MacMillan, Inc., 1986.

Moreno, Richard. *The Nevada Trivia Book*. Baldwin Park, CA: Gem Guides Book Company, 1998.

Moriarty, Noah. *Modern Marvels: Las Vegas Hotels*. Produced by Actuality Productions Inc. for A&E Television Networks, New York, New York, 1997.

Murbarger, Nell. *Ghosts of the Glory Trail*. Los Angeles: Westernlore Press, 1956.

Murphy, Virginia Reed. *Across the Plains in the Donner Party: A Personal Narrative of the Overland Trip to California 1846-47*. Silverthorne, CO: VistaBooks, 1995.

Nielsen, Norm. *Tales of Nevada,* Reno: Tales of Nevada Publications, 1989.

Nielsen, Norm. *Tales of Nevada, Volume 2*. Reno: Tales of Nevada Publications, 1990.

Noeth, Louise Ann. *The Drama in the Desert*. http://roadsters.com/louise.html, 1997-1999.

Powers, Francis Gary with Curt Gentry. *Operation Overflight: The U-2 Spy Pilot Tells His Story for the First Time*. New York: Holt, Rhinehart, and Winston, 1970.

Reed, Laurence, editor. *Las Vegas and the Mormons*. Produced by Lion Television Production for BBC/A&E Network Co-Production, 1998.

Robertson, Frank C. and Beth Kay Harris. *Boom Towns of the Great Basin*. Denver: Sage Books, 1962.

Rogers, Keith. "Damage from worst floods parallels growth." *Las Vegas Review-Journal*, July 9, 1999.

Roske, Ralph J. *Las Vegas: A Desert Paradise*. Tulsa: Continental Heritage Press, Inc., 1986.

Schoenmann, Joe and Keith Rogers. "Clinton OKs disaster funds." *Las Vegas Review-Journal*, July 21, 1999.

Settle, Mary Lund, and Raymond W. Settle. *Saddles & Spurs: The Pony Express Saga*. Lincoln: University of Nebraska Press, 1972, originally published 1955, by the Stackpole Company.

Sheehan, Jack, ed. *The Players: The Men Who Made Las Vegas*. Reno: University of Nevada Press, 1997.

Sprenger-Farley, Terri. *The Great Train Robbery*. Carson City, NV: Nevada Magazine, May/June 1986.

Stept, Stephen. *The American Experience: Hoover Dam*. Produced by Firstlight Pictures for the WGBH Educational Foundation, Boston, 1999.

Stewart, George R. *Ordeal by Hunger: The Story of the Donner Party*. New York: Houghton-Mifflin, 1988, originally published 1936.

"The Story of The Hoover Dam." *Compressed Air Magazine*. Las Vegas: Nevada Publications, 1931-35.

Thompson, David. *Nevada: A History of Changes*. Reno: Grace Dangberg Foundation, 1986.

Titus, A. Costandina. *Bombs in the Backyard: Atomic Testing and American Politics*. Reno: University of Nevada Press, 1986.

Weatherford, Mike. "Shows cannot go on after storm." *Las Vegas Review-Journal*, July 9, 1999.

Wheeler, Sessions S. *The Desert Lake: The Story of Nevada's Pyramid Lake*. Caldwell, ID: The Caxton Printers Ltd., 1987.

Wilhelm, Walt. *Last Rig to Battle Mountain*. New York: William Morrow & Company, Inc.: 1970.

Wright, Harold Bell. *The Winning of Barbara Worth*. Gretna, LA: Pelican Publishing Company, 1999. Originally published 1911.

Zanjani, Sally. *Goldfield: The Last Gold Rush on the Western Frontier*. Athens, OH: Swallow Press/Ohio University Press, 1992.

Zapler, Mike. "Flood control measures avert worse damage." *Las Vegas Review-Journal*, July 11, 1999.

Zeff, Lisa, Executive Producer, Pete Simmons, Producer, Ralph A Peck, Editor. *On the Inside: Hoover Dam*. ABCNews Productions, 1997.

Index

About the Author

Elizabeth Gibson got hooked on reading and writing at about the age of thirteen. She became interested in history when she read the "Bicentennial Series" by John Jakes. In college she combined these interests as she pursued a double major in English and history. Elizabeth began a career as a freelancer when she researched place name origins in eastern Washington. Her articles have appeared in several local publications and online. She has worked as a technical writer for a government contractor for more than fifteen years.